PARTIES

FOR OLDER CHILDREN

Angela Hollest

Penelope Gaine

To David, Edward and Clare
and Michael, David and Daniel

Acknowledgements
We would like to thank Christine Curzon, who
typed the manuscript (again and again!), as
well as our very generous friends and their
children, who gave us so much vital information,
especially Anna, Nick and Vivienne, Rosie, Delia,
Cherry, Melissa, Maggie, Sue, Pam and Trish.

By the same authors
CHILDREN'S PARTIES

First published in 1986 by
Judy Piatkus (Publishers) Limited, London

British Library Cataloguing in Publication Data

Hollest, Angela
    Parties for older children.
    1. Children's parties
    I. Title   II. Gaine, Penelope
    793.2'1   GV1205

    ISBN 0-86188-396-9
    ISBN 0-86188-540-6 Pbk

Edited by Susan Fleming
Designed by Dave Allen
Special photography by Ron Sutherland

Phototypeset in 11/12½ Linotron Trade Gothic Light
Printed and bound in Great Britain by
The Bath Press, Avon

Contents

Introduction

'I am never giving another party!' We know the feeling! But if you use this book, it should help you through all the minefields so that you can give a party which *everyone* can enjoy. Between the ages of eight and fourteen, children begin to grow up (and parents to grow old!), and if this means a delicious new taste of independence for children, it should mean the same for parents too. However, it's not quite so simple, and there are problems ahead, which is why we decided this book was needed. We have only been able to write it because of our own experiences and because so many generous friends, children and adults alike, have passed on their tips, traumas, and triumphs! It is, we hope, a comprehensive and well-tried guide, and all our suggestions can be adapted to suit your lifestyle.

We have included in the first part of the book many ideas for different types of parties. If you are holding a disco party – don't be appalled at the thought – follow the plan of campaign and you will come through with flying colours. Discuss with your children how your ideas and theirs can sensibly be reconciled, and remember *both* sides must be prepared to listen and be reasonable. We give hints for large-scale party venues, invitations, decorations, plus ideas for food (with shopping-list quantities) and drinks, including the to-be and not-to-be of alcohol for the older age group.

Smaller supper and dinner parties can be quickly organised. If you want to have a theme, there are suggestions on suitable invitations, decorations and mad party food and drink (from pink chicken to green cocktails!). Incorporate a mini disco or play some of the hilarious games that we describe.

Daytime events can be just as enjoyable. Have a match party – football, cricket, rounders, tennis, swimming, etc – or play outdoor games, including an assault course or bike gymkhana. The competitive spirit need not be too obvious – run the party efficiently and it will be great fun even for the less games-minded children. Provide one of our scrumptious teas and lunches or give a sizzling barbecue.

Take a group of friends on an outing party – skating, swimming, etc – or you could go to watch soccer, horse shows, a performance at the theatre, or the animals at a safari park. We give you masses of suggestions, together with do-it-yourself menus for picnics and snacks, or where to go if you want to stop off with a crowd of children. There are plenty of car games to keep you all busy en route.

Another form of party is a family get-together, and you should always involve the children: they can help to set the table or choose and even cook the food – nothing grand, our motto being 'Keep it simple'! Use Hogmanay, Hallowe'en, Guy Fawkes, the Grand National, half-term – anything as an excuse for a party with your own or with other families.

All the recipes for food and drinks are in the second half of the book. Always try and prepare as much of the food as you can ahead of the party. There is a huge choice – decide from the menu in the text what you want to serve, and then turn to the back of the book when you come to the nitty-gritty of cooking. Don't panic! We keep it simple – we are mothers too. We also have a huge section on fun drinks, obviously mostly non-alcoholic. However, there are some others for older children's parties if required. There are also a few ideas for home-made sweets, which could serve as prizes or going-home presents.

Children's parties need not be an extravagant luxury. They can be organised without vast expense, and they do have a function. They teach children to socialise easily, to relax with adults and contemporaries, and to have a giggle, letting their hair down, but still under control. As children get older they will learn to introduce friends to one another, to make sure everyone is enjoying themselves, and not to be hyper-sensitive if they are not invited to a party down the road! You can't always invite everyone.

Keep a party file and include information re addresses and ages of guests, ideas you used for parties, and food you have served. It will be invaluable for future reference, especially if you want ideas for younger children. It's so hard to remember what you did, when, and for how many, etc – and if a friend of ours had not kept such a file some important hints would not have been included in this book.

Our aim has been to give you all a practical, diverse and economical, but above all, *fun* party book. Have a great time!

Angela Hollest
Penelope Gaine
May 1986

Disco Parties

If you are thinking of giving a large party, why not share the strain and give a joint one with friends? You can then pool ideas, skills and guests. This is particularly helpful if you want to have boys and girls but don't know too many children of the opposite sex to your child. So long as the hosts and hostesses all get on together, and are the same age group, it is actually great fun for them too. Giving this type of party is not particularly cheap, however, and dividing the cost is another incentive for sharing the occasion. However, if you want to hold a smaller disco party for younger children, incorporate it with a supper party (see page 21).

Party Preparations

VENUE

One of the main drawbacks of sharing a party is deciding on a venue. In many ways a totally independent hall or club that you could use is the ideal if the party is to be a large one. However, if you are planning to use one of the hosts' homes, then remember that it is inevitable that the guests will tend to think of the party as being given by those whose home it is. To help the others feel involved, why not let the replies to the invitations be sent to their houses? But *do* make sure that there is no confusion as to where the party will eventually be held by wording the invitation very clearly.

If you are giving the party in a hired hall you will probably need to book it very early, so find out who is in charge of running the place and contact them before doing anything else (see also page 11). It is probably best to avoid weekends and hold the party on a week night in the holidays, as your hall will be more likely to be available in the week, and it may help also to avoid gatecrashers.

Other points to remember are to check that the electrics are suitable for a discothèque, and also to ensure that the heating or ventilation (if the party is in the summer) are both adequate. Look at the kitchen and equipment, and especially the hot water supply. Make a list of the things you will need to bring with you (see page 19 for check list). Check the cloakroom facilities too. Don't forget to ask the caretaker at what time you will be able to get into the hall to prepare the decorations, transport food, etc. Also enquire about insurance for the hall.

We do not suggest that you put up large notices advertising that your party is being held in the building, as gatecrashers can be a problem. If you are in the country and people are coming from a long way away, why not photocopy an Ordnance Survey map. Or simply send diagrams to show your guests exactly where the party is being held.

If possible, choose a hall that is not too near a pub. If you do have to, then make sure a father can 'police' outside the hall to avoid gatecrashers and boys going from the party to the pub to buy drinks. It's amazing what they can get up to!

In many ways it is preferable, and of course

cheaper, to have your party at home, depending on the numbers you have invited. Even garages and barns can be transformed with some imaginative decorations, although you can still hit problems. Is the room large enough to accommodate equipment, children and noise? Is the electricity supply suitable for whatever form of music you are using, whether a group, disco or someone's hi-fi, and lighting? Similarly, can you heat whatever room you choose if necessary, and if it rains, is it feasible to transport food, plates, etc, etc? Remember you will need space for serving tables (for food and bar) as well as the disco.

If you don't have outside lighting to show the way to the party room, night lights in jam jars (see page 57) will be perfectly adequate, so long as you have someone available to replenish them if necessary and so long as it doesn't pour with rain! Have some torches to hang up if necessary. Also, you can buy (but they are expensive) very effective garden flares.

Another problem which might arise by having your party at home is that of neighbours being disturbed. This can probably be overcome by a diplomatic warning and perhaps a small box of chocs being presented prior to the event. Give some truffles or fudge (see page 122) made by the children – very endearing.

When it comes to teenage parties, many people experience problems if they hold the party in their house. The larger the party, obviously the more difficulties there can be. This is not to say that every party is going to turn into a disaster, far from it. However, it is only fair on both parents and children to face the fact that sometimes guests get carried away and do not respect other people's property and homes as parents expect they should. There is no point in causing mammoth rows and frustrations between children and

parents over something which should have been great fun. So get together before the party and really discuss with your children what has happened at other parties they have been to, and what opinion they have of giving the party in their own home. We think it is up to the parents to remember what they got up to when they were young and be tolerant, and up to the children to understand that parents are only expecting reasonable behaviour and not trying to be fuddy-duddies. If holding the party in the garage saves a wrecked carpet, frayed tempers, and means everyone wants another party next year, then forego the comforts of having it in the sitting room.

This is not meant to sound all gloom and doom! Be prepared and it will never happen!

THE DISCOTHÈQUE

If your children have been to plenty of local disco parties, they will probably know who will provide the very best music. Maybe some elder brother runs a disco as a hobby. This would no doubt be a lot cheaper than a professional, but don't forget that it will be the music and the disco that make the party and it would be a false economy to spoil the event by choosing the wrong one. Check the following points when initially booking:

1. If you are holding your party at home, you may find that a room you thought was perfectly adequate in size might be quite unsuitable – for example, the ceiling might be too low, and the noise of the discothèque might therefore be unbearable. Do discuss the size of the room and the amount of space the actual equipment will require, to see whether it is feasible or not.

2. Check that the electrics you can provide are suitable. If the venue is in a garage, for instance, then it is probably best if the disc jockey comes and inspects the system to check everything is correct, well in advance of the event.

3. Ask what he will be bringing in the way of extras – a strobe, a bubble machine etc – and what the extras will cost.

4. Discuss the age group you are entertaining. The disc jockey is the one who will have to keep the party going, and when the children are young, up to the age of about ten, it may be worth including the odd game like Disco Knees or Islands (see page 18).

5. Check on the time that the disc jockey will arrive before the party starts.

6. Check that he knows the way. Give him a map if there is *any* query.

7. Write everything down that you discuss and send a letter confirming the arrangements, having taken a copy first.

8. Query whether you may have to provide a deposit on booking the disco. Also check his insurance.

PARTY THEMES

Having organised your venue and the disco, probably the next most important thing to do is to decide whether you are having a theme for your party. This can affect the invitations, decorations and food. It seems that the older the children get, the less likely they are to enjoy any sort of dressing-up at parties. However, you can have themes which involve whatever degree of dressing up they want – a Black and White party, Razzle Dazzle, Dress to Impress, Dress to Dazzle, St Trinians, Glitter and Gleam, Outrageous Dress, Funky Punk, Shimmer and Shine, Down and Outs, Red, White and Blue, Multicoloured, 1920s, 1950s, Gender Bender, Horror party, etc . Don't forget seasonal parties, for example a Red and Green Christmas party, Dress to Sparkle for Guy Fawkes, Spooky Spoofs and Ghosts and Ghouls for Hallowe'en; Valentine parties are good as well.

Up to about the age of eleven, children will not mind dolling themselves up but will want to know what everyone else is wearing, so do make that clear on your invitation. Remember what you would have felt like if you had been sent off to a party in the wrong clothes at that age!

After about eleven you will probably find that they will not 'dress up' in the same way. This is up to you and your children to organise between you – the children will know what's what! They will keep you up to date on what's new; ideas date so quickly that you should always be prepared to take advice from the young.

INVITATIONS

If you are giving a large party don't forget how time-consuming it is to write out all the invitations. Remember how long it takes to do all those Christmas cards! If you are sharing this party then maybe you will all decide to take on a certain number each, or perhaps one person who isn't very good at making decorations, say, could organise all the invitations and someone else do the decorations, etc but that is up to all of you to decide. Obviously the children can be roped in and may like to undertake the invitations themselves. If they have time, then that is fine, but do all of you go through the shortlist and check the envelopes off, before final posting. Make sure that, if the venue and the RSVP addresses are different, this is very clear. You don't want half the party arriving at an empty house.

Even if a lot of the invitations will be handed out at school, have all the addresses and, if possible, telephone numbers written down in case of a drama. One small point: when we have shared parties, we did agree that if one of the hosts (children that is) was ill, the others would carry on with the party. This obviously depends on the venue and circumstances, but do discuss it between yourselves beforehand so that there are no misunderstandings.

While preparing your guest list, remember not to mix the ages too much. You would probably find that twelve-year-olds would not be pleased to find masses of nine-year-olds at the same party! Think back – you would not have invited many three-year-olds to a six-year-old's tea party. The principle still applies! Keep two separate lists of boys and girls with clear columns to tick who is coming and who is not. You can see quickly and clearly how numbers are going. Always invite some extra boys anyway.

DATE PITFALLS
The decision of when to hold the party will probably dictate how many children will be on your initial guest list. For example, giving a party in the summer holidays can be a real problem and you may want to ask extra numbers to allow for many children being away. August is obviously the worst month of all – there could be a one-third refusal rate – so if possible it is best to plan for a date near to everybody going back to school. There is quite an exodus too in the Easter holidays, now that so many schools and families go skiing then, so check carefully before choosing a date. The Christmas holidays have a natural party atmosphere and in many ways it is the best time to give a party, but remember that you will have Christmas to cope with too, so unless you are ultra-efficient or going away for Christmas itself, we suggest you hold the party at the very beginning, or end, of the holidays.

Always try and check as best you can that there isn't going to be another major school or local event that would coincide and diminish your numbers. It's always better for a disco to seem a bit crowded, so do invite enough people to fill your room.

THE INVITATIONS THEMSELVES
Perhaps your children have specific ideas as to what they want their invitations to look like. Do persuade them to be practical. An elaborate design done by hand may be fine for the smaller event, but if you are contemplating inviting well over 100 children the exercise will become tedious! One way around that problem is to design a single invite and then photocopy it. (Local libraries or office stationers offer this service.) If the photocopy paper is flimsy then make it into a stand-up card rather than a single piece of paper, and remember to allow for this when taking your photocopies. The children could either draw or stencil designs on the corners, or wherever they choose. After the invitations have been printed they could

David & Tim invite you to a

Tennis Party in the park at 4.30

Bring your kit

★ CLARE CLARKE AND EDWARD JAMES ☆ invite you to a

SPARKLING PARTY

at 1, The Priory

Dress to Dazzle Supper

on Thursday 1st September 7.30 pm until 11.30 pm

RSVP 4 St Helen's Trumpington

either cut the edges with pinking shears or put some clear light adhesive (Bostik) on the paper and sprinkle it with glitter.

Printed invitations are obviously the least trouble, but more expensive. Go to local printers or phone up through the Yellow Pages and get quotes. Go down with your children to decide what typeface, colour and type of card you require (if you have a colour theme to your party, try to marry up the colour here). Take with you an ordinary postcard on which you have formulated all the information you wish to include. It is possible to have a rough copy printed, so that you can look at it and double-check that everything is correct before the final print is run off. It costs a bit extra but might save you having to alter every invitation. Obviously, you will be asking more children than you expect to come to the party, but order more invitations than guests you intend to invite: whoever writes the invitations will probably make the odd mistake, and you might also think of some extra guests after the other invitations have been sent out.

Check that the size of the card will fit a POP (Post Office Preferred) standard envelope so that you can buy envelopes easily, and at a reasonable price.

TIMING

It seems easiest to plan your party timing backwards, so that if it ends early it should start sooner, and vice versa. Deciding on the time a party ends is a very personal matter, and if it is an oldest child's party one is somehow more aware that it is long past bedtime! (As the eldest often moans, life is much easier for the younger children as parents' attitudes soften!) If the party is for young children – say ten-year-olds – and especially if it is in term-time, then you will probably feel that 10 o'clock is late enough, so start at about 7 pm. Once the children are older, it can be later; as you are bothering to have the party at all, you might as well make it a late night, starting at 8 pm, say, and going on until midnight. Children hate to feel different and while we must not be governed by what others do, we should be sensitive to a child's feelings. If you are worried that it will all end too late, then leave the idea until next year and give an 'outing' party instead (see page 44).

DECORATIONS

No doubt you will have your own ideas about decorating your party room but here are a few general hints and ideas as guidelines. Don't forget that once the disco lighting is in full swing the decorations will not be as important as they appear in the cold light of day. However, your venue can be made to look attractive and fun without too much hassle. If you are having a theme to your party then tie in the decorations with this.

Make your decorations well in advance and have them sorted out ready to put up on the day, or the day before the party. It takes a lot longer than one imagines to plan, design and construct decorations, so leave yourselves sufficient time.

In general, if you are having your party in a hall, then consider the following:

1. How long beforehand will you have to decorate the room? You can't go mad if you only have two hours before the party starts.
2. Don't worry about the lighting if you are hiring a professional disco; they will provide their own lights and can hire extra ones if you think you need them.
3. If the hall is large remember that small decorations will not show up effectively.
4. The wall surface of your venue will determine what you can or want to put on it. Consider the size of the walls and the height of the ceiling when planning your decorations.
5. Have plenty of Blu-Tack, which is good as it does not damage wall surfaces if treated correctly. Double-sided sticky tape is very useful but do not use this on wall surfaces which would be damaged by the tape as it is extremely strong (although it does not stick well to wooden beams). Depending on whether or not it is appropriate to use them, have good strong drawing pins to hand. Remember to take a couple of pairs of scissors when you are putting your decorations up.

Posters. Maybe you could find suitable posters that are appropriate to your party theme. Or there is fantastic wrapping paper around which you could use instead.

Balloons. You can hang balloons around the room in clusters. Spray them with glitter for extra dazzle. Tie these clusters together with pieces of parcel ribbon with strands hanging down (about 2 feet or 60 cm). Take a pair of scissors and run the back of them down the long strands, one at a time, very firmly, and the ribbon will go into curls and twirls. Suspend the clusters wherever you want.

If the ceiling is high and you want to make the atmosphere more 'cosy', see if it would be possible to string up vegetable netting as a balloon net and fill this with balloons. If you wish, and depending on the floor surface and the type of party, mix some balloons with water in them amongst the ordinary balloons. The balloons will all be stamped on at the end of the party, and our children thought it was very amusing when they went to a disco where this had been done! Do *not* fill the balloons with water too soon before the party as they sometimes burst more easily with the water in them. Be prepared for some wise guy to let down the balloons before the end of the party – either you mustn't mind, or make the net so difficult to undo that only you know the combination lock!

If you have a party shop near you (see Yellow Pages), you may be able to get hold of helium-filled balloons. These will be quite expensive but they are fun and if you have them as a centre piece floating up from a crossbeam they can look very attractive. They are usually foil on one side at least, so reflect the light well. If you are having a Valentine party then try and get hold of heart-shaped ones – remember them flying behind the Prince and Princess of Wales as they went off on their honeymoon?

Streamers. Don't ignore good old streamers, especially if you are having a colour theme. To save buying expensive streamers, you can easily make them out of crêpe paper. This is a very cheap way of decorating a large room, and the children can have great fun making them. Buy packets of crêpe paper – the amount and colour depending on your plans – and keep the paper folded as it is. Cut it across into 2 inch (5 cm) strips, then frill the edges by running the back of a pair of scissors down either side. Unwind the strips, join ends with double-sided sticky tape (expensive, but extremely strong and durable). Twist the strips and fasten around the walls and across the ceiling with Blu-Tack. (Try to put these decorations away carefully after the party – they may come in handy next time.)

Why not throw the very thin (and cheap) streamers which curl when you throw them over the streamers crossing the ceiling? You can buy these in packets of about eight from stationers' shops.

Coloured Card or Foil Shapes. These can be cut out into whichever shape you feel appropriate to your party, and Blu-Tacked to the walls and, if possible, the ceiling perhaps. A friend's daughter cut out huge hands and feet and stuck them all over the walls; as you can imagine, the footprints looked marvellous on the ceiling! If you were trying to decorate a very large hall this could be quite time-consuming and expensive to execute, and would be more appropriate, perhaps, in a garage or similar-sized room. However, use your imagination and choose whatever shape marries in with your theme, if you have one: for example, stars, moons and witches' hats for Hallowe'en; hearts for Valentines, etc.

If you are going to try and suspend foil shapes from the ceiling you would have to stiffen the foil because otherwise it would curl in the heat of the disco. Do this by gluing the foil to thin card. Alternatively, cover one wall completely with foil (if it's not too big) as this looks wonderful with the lights. Some dairies are happy to lend you the long strips of foil left over from making bottle tops, if you promise to return them the next day. With their cut-out holes, these are very decorative (and free!) and glitter in the lights.

Painted Branches or Twigs. It is very easy to emulsion-paint or spray-paint bare branches or twigs. If you wanted to fill an empty corner, put a branch (painted in whatever colour your party theme requires) into a tub, and use bricks to hold it in position. Fill the tub with sand. If the branch is very tall and still not 100 per cent secure, tie fishing line to it and attach to the wall on both sides to hold it in position.

Your branch can be decorated in any number of ways. Foil shapes can be made: cut two identical shapes from foil and glue these on to card of the same shape to avoid them curling in the heat. Make a hole at the top and thread cotton ties through to suspend it from the branch. You can also cut kitchen foil into strips long enough to tie into bows – the length will depend on the size you want the bows to be. Tie these bows all over the branches. You can use your Christmas tinsel on the 'tree' plus lights if you want and, of course, if you're giving a Christmas disco you must have a decorated tree in the room – it really adds to the atmosphere.

Food and Drink

The age of the children determines the type and amount of food you will provide, as well as its method of serving. Younger children will

A. Menu for the Youngest Age Group (per plate)

4 cocktail sausages
1 small packet crisps
A small handful nuts
1 satsuma (if Christmas time)
Half mini bridge roll
1 cheese straw boat with sail
1 cube cheese on stick
1 mini eclair
1 mini filled meringue

Break-time   Ice cream in cornet

B. Menu for the 'In-Betweens' (per plate)

1 chicken drumstick
2 cocktail sausages
3 cucumber sticks (3 inches or 7.5 cm long)
4 carrot sticks (3 inches or 7.5 cm long)
1 ham roll
1 packet crisps
2 cheese squares
1 finger pizza (cold)
Container of apples, bananas, seedless grapes
or satsumas
1 chocolate mousse

Break-time
Vanilla cornet with flakes

C. Menu for the Older Group

From about the age of twelve there is a change of atmosphere at parties, and instead of giving the children individual plates they like to help themselves to finger food from a main table, which they will want to wander up to as and when they choose. As with the other menus, check first with your children to see what sort of things they want. From about fourteen onwards you will find that the children want very little food indeed. You will have to be guided by them. Hopefully guests will have had supper beforehand, but if you are serving any alcohol it is wise to have nibbles available in case anyone has not eaten.

Cheese and pineapple on sticks (2 per person)
Twiglets (2 large bowls)
Tiny meringues (2 each)
Cocktail sausages on sticks (4 each)
Crudités (carrots and celery sticks,
cauliflower florets)
Ritz biscuits
Dips: Tomato, curry, horseradish
Pizza fingers (1 finger each)
Pitta bread and pâté (1 small piece each)
Crisps (2 large bowls)
Chocolate praline cake (1 square each)
Container of satsumas (winter)
Large bowl of strawberries (summer)

eat more and stop for supper, while older ones will eat far less but will nibble away throughout the evening. The amounts we give can be adapted easily to whatever size of party you are planning. (And don't panic at the thought of large-scale catering: it is *not* horrendous, as you will see!) Remember that the disco organiser and your helpers will want to have some sustenance too, so include them when you calculate your requirements.

We suggest Menu A or B for younger children up to eleven, and Menu C for an older party. For the younger age groups we also suggest including a break – when you serve ice cream cornets to everyone. The older children will definitely *not* require this.

It is so difficult to be specific about age so ask your children what they would like. Older teenagers really are not interested in food, but as fussy mother-hens we recommend you always provide something, especially if there is any alcohol being served.

Up to the ages of eleven to twelve, the children should stop for a supper and to give everyone a breather. We think it is far easier to give each child a paper plate with their food already on it. This avoids long queues building up as each child chooses what he or she wants to eat. You may have some waste, but it's worth that for the ease. The main problem is that you may well not have sufficient space to lay out all the plates, but so long as you have a certain number ready, helpers can be assembling others while you are serving. If you are organised, it will all go smoothly.

You will need tables on which to lay out food, whatever the age group. Place your tables where you – and the guests – can get at them easily. If the party is taking place in one room (which is best so as not to split it up), then put the tables along one wall. Make them look attractive with brightly coloured coverings – tablecloths, plastic cloths or coloured sheets. If the table surfaces are likely to be damaged, cover them first with a polythene or plastic sheet (dustbin bags sticky-taped together will be fine).

These disco party menus have been tried and tested and proved popular, but obviously your children may have a particular favourite which you would like to include. The lists on the previous page are what we suggest you put on each plate. In the recipe section (pages 74–78) we say what quantity you will need to buy for fifty guests, and give individual recipes for anything that needs cooking. Think small in everything – the eclairs, for instance, should be tiny two-mouthful ones. This means that food is easier to handle and the plate doesn't look over-loaded. You can have some plates at the back with extra sausages, cheese straws or whatever for the odd child who might not feel like eating much at suppertime but who, as confidence grows during the evening, suddenly regains an appetite!

DRINKS

Children get through a lot of drink at a disco party and you should always provide plenty. Obviously you will serve non-alcoholic drinks to the younger children. It would be easy to say, 'Right, no alcohol at *any* children's party, and that's it', but life is never that simple! Older children see their parents drinking, and so know that drink is part of the adult world which they feel they are ready to join. It depends on how you feel about alcohol as to what your opinion is on serving children even mildly alcoholic drinks. However, if you are having a party, the following tips should help you cope with this dilemma. Recipes can be found on pages 116–122.

1. Never give a party without adults in attendance – even if they are not always in the room. If you are serving alcoholic drink it is a good idea for a father to run the bar, to keep control of how much is served, to see, and to be seen.

2. Serve a 'cup' type drink, where you can control the content. If you are including alcohol for older children, you can cut this down after the first drink and it won't be noticed. (One friend kept lots of empty wine bottles on view!)

Have plenty of cut fruit in it – apple, orange, cucumber, lemon slices etc – and, depending on the time of year, mint leaves and strawberries. If you are having a very big party use either large plastic containers, preserving pans or new plastic buckets to mix your drink in. Have a large bowl to serve it in and use ladles to spoon it into the glasses. If you are having a small party, serve from a jug.

3. Always serve Coke, lemonade and orange squash as an alternative to a concoction. Put fruit in the orange jug to make it look more fun.

4. Buy a non-alcoholic sparkling wine, and either use this on its own in a wine-cup, or half and half with ordinary wine. Non-alcoholic drinks are becoming increasingly popular, whether wines or lagers.

5. In the interests of the party spirit, give your drinks intriguing names: we have used names for our recipes which are usually given to more alcoholic drinks (everyone will enjoy the sophistication even if they are not entirely convinced!) Adapt names for your concoctions to fit your party – Disco Dazzler or Super Spritzer, for instance.

6. Have masses of ice prepared. If your freezer is full of party food get a couple of friends to make you plenty and keep it for you in their freezers until the evening. Use a cold box if you are in a hired hall and have no freezer available. Have one or two ice containers on the 'bar' with some tongs for children to put their own ice in their drinks. If you are giving a large party, four large plastic carrier bags full of ice should provide enough for fifty.

7. You may find the following information useful. At a disco party for sixty-four eleven-year-olds recently, the Harvest Punch recipe was served, and approximately $112\frac{1}{4}$ pints (64 litres) of drink were consumed! The amounts were for the following mix. First of all, it was 1 cider to 2 apple juices and 5 lemonades;

followed by no cider, 3 apple juices and 5 lemonades.

The total quantities were: Lemonade, 24 bottles ($1\frac{1}{2}$ litres); Cider, 1 bottle ($1\frac{1}{2}$ litres); Apple juice, 15 boxes (1 litre).

In addition: Coke, 6 bottles ($1\frac{1}{2}$ litres); Orange squash, 2 jugs.

Far more drink was available (on a sale or return basis), and we would certainly advise you to have more than the above. However, it is interesting that drink averages $2\frac{1}{2}$ pints (1 litre) per child for an all-evening, energetic party. When they are older they will probably drink even more.

8. If you have older children coming, even if you think they are totally reliable, lock away *all* your own bottles of drinks (especially the spirits) and try to let the word be circulated that anyone bringing their own drinks will be sent home. Yes, we know it would be difficult to frisk them for hip flasks but keep an eye open. The most common way of trouble starting at teenage parties is when drinks *you* provide are laced with drinks that *they* provide. Give them a good cup to get them going, then lessen the alcohol and serve carefully with a very watchful eye from the barman, Dad. Have Coke and squash available as well of course.

9. Always have drinks delivered at least a day before your party, especially if you are having a large party when drinks will be heavy and bulky to move about. If you are hiring a hall or whatever, see if they can be delivered there on the morning of the party, depending on security at the venue. Remember that you can hire glasses from wine merchants if necessary. The advantage of using a wine merchant is that you can have everything on a sale or return basis, very useful for a large party. You don't want to run out of drinks or have to buy far more than you use. Confirm your order when you know the numbers.

Dancing Games

These are *not* for the consumption of older groups; leave them well alone to do their own thing! When the children are young and go to disco parties, it may help to break the ice if you have the odd game with mini Mars bars, or similar little treats, as prizes. We feel you should have an experienced disc jockey to cope with the younger age group; he will know if games are necessary and when to introduce them. Let him be in charge of the evening. He may well have suggestions of his own for games, so discuss this aspect of the party beforehand and supply him with the prizes. However, don't worry if you feel more should be happening and it isn't. The children will enjoy being left to their own devices, and will let themselves be guided by the disc jockey.

The children will probably stand around a bit. Don't panic! You will also find that they dance without having a 'partner' when they're younger. If you want to pair people up before playing a game, have a Paul Jones or a Shoe Dance first. Some games don't need the children to be paired off.

For the youngest group you may want to incorporate a few ordinary party games while the disc jockey has a breather. Choose from the selection on page 61, and don't forget to include the 'props' you will need for these on your checklist.

SHOE DANCE
Every girl puts one of her shoes in the centre. Each boy chooses a shoe and has to dance with whoever is his Cinderella.

DISCO DANCING COMPETITION
Just play a few disco records and the winners are the couple dancing the best according to the disc jockey.

PAUL JONES
The girls make a circle on the inside and the boys on the outside. The two circles move around in opposite directions to the music. When the music stops the boy and girl facing each other dance together.

DISCO KNEES
Everyone dances around and when the music stops the girl has to sit on the boy's knee without her feet touching the ground. If they do, or if she falls over, that couple is out.

MUSICAL ISLANDS
You will need to have a newspaper per couple for this game. Put the newspapers on the floor; when the music stops each couple has to jump on to an 'island'. Take away a newspaper each time, as in musical chairs.

NEWSPAPER GAME
You will need to supply a newspaper per couple. Get the boy to carry the newspaper while he is dancing. When the music stops, each couple stands on their own newspaper, which at that stage should be folded in half. The next time the music stops they have to fold the paper in half again before getting on to it. Each time the music stops they have to fold their paper into a smaller and smaller piece. The couple who wins are the last to stand on their paper without falling off.

TORCH DANCE
Give your disc jockey a torch. He can suddenly turn it on to someone, and they will be out.

FORFEIT DANCE

Prepare a list of forfeits prior to your party and give this to the disc jockey who can then make a forfeit dance as and when he wants. Forfeits can include anyone wearing a safety pin, anyone whose Christian name begins with a G, etc, etc. Those who are 'guilty' are out.

THE HOT POTATO

Give the disc jockey a balloon. The balloon has to be thrown about between the dancers as they are dancing. If the music stops and they have the balloon in their hands they are out. You will have to insist that they catch the balloon if it is thrown at them. If you see them deliberately not handling a balloon they will have to be out in any case.

STATUE DANCE

When the music stops the children have to stand absolutely still. Those who move are out.

DIAMONDS, HEARTS, SPADES AND CLUBS

Have four corners labelled as one of the four suits; have an adult standing at each one holding up a large home-made card, or pin up a card at each corner. When the music stops, the children go to whichever corner they choose. The disc jockey turns his back when the music stops and then shouts out one of the suits. The children in that corner are out. The game continues until there's only one child left on the floor.

Checklist

If you are having your party away from home you will need a checklist. Obviously you can discount some of the items given below if the venue is well equipped but it is probably worth flicking through the list anyway, just to check that you have thought of everything.

Decoration	Chopping board
Blu-Tack	Washing-up bowl
Food	Washing-up liquid
Drink	Towels
Corkscrews	Drying-up cloths
Can openers	J-cloths
Cutlery	Kitchen roll
Crockery	Paper napkins

Ice, tongs and ice bucket
Cold box – to keep spare ice in
Scissors – for cutting cartons, etc.
Dustpan, brush and broom, bin liners
Matches, if gas stove or heating system
Large jugs, bowls, etc, for drinks
Large bucket for slops if 'bar' not near sink
Ladies – for serving drinks
Glasses (can be hired, or use plastic)
Polythene covers, if necessary to cover table
    surface before putting on cloths (sellotape
    dry cleaning bags together, PVC tablecloths,
    groundsheets, etc, for either bar or serving
    tables)

Disc jockey's telephone number

For younger children's disco parties only

Props if needed, and prizes for the games; camera and flash.

Items for girl's loo

Tissues	Cotton wool
Perfume	Spare loo rolls
Hairspray	First-aid kit
Comb	

Supper and Dinner Parties

Evening parties take over from tea parties as children get older. Supper or dinner parties are greatly enjoyed by girls on their own from eight to about eleven years old: they appreciate the details of candles, flowers and pretty food. A vital ingredient is darkness, so when they are younger it is probably best not to plan this for summertime. Give a barbecue instead (see page 67). Older children would prefer a more sophisticated mixed party. (Before going on to late discos or teenage balls, it would be fun to invite some friends for dinner and then go together to the party.)

When discussing how many to invite, remember that you will have to fit everybody in without too much squash. Smaller parties can be just as much fun, and sometimes children may prefer to invite just their closest friends. When you come to the mixed dinner party, numbers will no doubt be decided between you and the children, but try and make sure that at least one 'life and soul of the party' is invited to get things going from the start!

For the eight-year-olds we think 6–8 or 8.30 pm is an ideal time span – and helpful if parents have to collect children before going out themselves. As they get older, 7.30–10 or 10.30 pm would be a suitable length of time, or make it an 'all-night' party: ask them to bring sleeping bags and stay the night with collection time at, say, 10 the next morning! Once they are into mixed parties then timing is up to you and the children to sort out together.

The recipes we give (see pages 78–101) serve eight, but it is simple enough to double the quantities if required. We have given lists of possible starters, main courses and puddings so that you and your children can choose anything that appeals to you, in whatever combination you require. If you feel, for example, that the younger children won't manage a starter *and* a main course, then adapt the ideas to whatever you and your family decide is appropriate. Only small amounts of a starter need be served; it is there to make the children feel they are having a proper dinner party. You may think that some of our starters sound rather sophisticated, but as children get older they will appreciate this. If in doubt, experiment on your own children first – and always discuss it with them anyway.

The drinks you provide will depend on the age group you are inviting. We give plenty of suggestions for 'concoction' recipes and for drinks to carry through your party themes (see page 117). Give whatever drink you serve a suitable name. Make coloured ice cubes for extra fun – remember they will melt so marry up the colour with your coloured drink. Add a few drops of food colouring to water before freezing the cubes.

Strike a sophisticated note with frosted glasses. To prepare these, beat up an egg white until it has lost its sticky quality, dip the rim of the glass first in the egg white and then immediately into a container of caster sugar and leave to dry. If you want to have coloured frosting, mix the sugar with a food colouring before dipping the glass – for example, add cochineal for the pink party. (The only problem with these glasses is that they are quite difficult to wash up!)

Buy little cocktail trimmings (from good stationers or party shops); mini paper sunshades; little plastic animals to hang on the edge of the glasses; plastic freezer shapes, like pink elephants, which you can use instead of ice cubes.

No doubt the children would like to organise a seating plan, and would enjoy making individual place cards for the guests. The design and colour of the cards could be tied in with the party theme or decorations. Perhaps they could do some fun menus to go on the table too.

Themes and decorations depend on the age group you are inviting. Always look around and utilise what you have at home – it is amazing how you forget what is tucked away at the back of a cupboard. This is particularly applicable if you decide to have a colour theme for your party.

For a supper party you will need helpers – the number will depend on how many you are inviting. Don't think you can organise games, be cook, waitress, disc jockey and cloakroom attendant all by yourself. No matter how organised you are beforehand, it is amazing how serving the food, doing the drinks and bringing in the next course becomes a real chore if you are on your own! Enlist some friends or older children to help. For the older children's mixed parties, they will serve and

clear themselves: all you have to do is leave them to it!

Don't forget that if an older mixed group don't know each other well, conversation may be a bit sticky. Try odd tricks to get them chatting: serve the Meat Fondue (see page 113) or finish off a meal with the Fruit Fondue (see page 101). Everyone has a giggle together then. And afterwards suggest a few games, such as the Dictionary Game, Charades (girls versus boys), Team Trivial Pursuits (see pages 64–66). Discuss this with your teenager in advance. As a last resort, show a video!

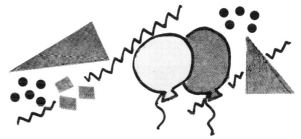

Candlelit Dinner Party

The younger age group are very appreciative of being allowed to feel sophisticated and grown up, so let them have a candlelit dinner. Make the table look pretty with candles and flowers. Serve uncomplicated food which most children would like a little bit of. Have a mini-disco, or play a few games before supper (see page 61) whilst everybody is arriving. After the meal you could continue playing games, or have a video, magician or another mini-disco to finish the evening off. Alternatively, make it a fancy-dress occasion like Hallowe'en.

If you want to give a small disco party for younger children you will need a clear area for them to dance in, and some good pop discs or tapes. Incorporate games with the dancing

MENU
CANDLELIT PARTY

Melon Balls or Cubes with Orange Juice
Cocktail Vol-au-Vents

★★★★★★★★★★

Spaghetti (or pasta curls and
shells) Bolognese
Shepherds' Pie Special
Chicken Pie
Mock Moussaka

★★★★★★★★★

Vegetables

★★★★★★★★★★

Snow Princess Cake
Pavlova with Cream and Fruit
Ice Cream Bombe
Chocolate Mousse
Lemon Mousse

Christmas fairy lights on a time switch so that they go on and off like disco lights, or simply change your ordinary electric light bulbs for coloured ones. Always keep your decorations in tune with your party theme if you have one.

Don't forget that with this age group you will need prizes for the games, and presents to take home. So be prepared (buy little novelties, mini Mars Bars, or make some sweets, see the section on presents at the back of the book).

As far as the food is concerned, try to have everything prepared by the afternoon. Remember these recipes are for eight, so adapt accordingly. Clingfilm will be invaluable to prevent everything drying out. Anything to be served hot can be heated up at the last minute. Avoid having to carve anything. Keep the food simple and choose dishes that can be 'doled' out, so that you can then help serve the vegetables. Always cook a few sausages, no matter what main course you have chosen, just in case there is a child who doesn't like it!

Pink Party

and the children will feel less inhibited and everyone can join in.

Decorate your room with streamers (see page 14 on how to make them) and balloons. Once you have blown up the balloons use a felt tipped pen and draw a funny face and write a child's name on each one. Tie a piece of string, wool, ribbon or parcel ribbon to each. Mix the balloons into bunches, tie the strings together into a slip knot. If the children are still young enough to appreciate taking a balloon home after a party you can easily free the balloons by pulling the end of the knot. If you want the balloons for decoration only, use parcel ribbon and then run the back of a pair of scissors firmly down the individual strands to form curls. Maybe you could rig up your

A pink party is probably more appropriate for girls on their own. You can really go to town making everything look extremely pretty and delicate. Obviously, you could change this slightly to become a pink and white party, and the advantage of a two-colour theme is that someone with very little in the way of pink clothing will probably have something white to which they can add pink ribbons or tights. Tell everyone to wear pink and send pink invitations using pink writing paper. Alternatively, use white paper and decorate and write it with pink felt-tip.

Pink and white crêpe streamers can be used to decorate the room: buy pink and white crêpe paper and make your own (see page 14). You could go to town and make some tissue paper flowers and decorate the table or part of the room with them. They are quite time-consuming to do but so pretty they are worth the effort! To make them you will need pink tissue paper, cake doilies (size depends on the size flowers you want) and thin wire, perhaps florists' wire. Cut the tissue into different-sized circles, place three or four layers on top of each other and put the doily underneath. Make a 'nob' with the end of a piece of the wire and push the other end through the paper layers. Form the paper layers into a cup or flower shape, and hold in place with the twisted wire or sticky tape.

Carry the theme through to the table decorations with pink candles, napkins, plates, etc. You can dye salt pink with some drops of cochineal and then dry it out in the airing cupboard (it will go a bit hard at first so just mix it up). Put it in an open salt cellar plus little spoon: use an egg cup if you've nothing else to so that the salt can be seen!

If you can run to the expense, put a few little pink and white flowers as a posy on the table: it need not be very big. Try to make the flowers

MENU
PINK PARTY

Wild Cherry Soup
Pink Prawn Pâté
Taramasalata
Pink Tomato Dip with Crisps or Crudités

★★★★★★★★★★★

Gammon with Redcurrant Jelly Sauce
Chicken with Pink Mayonnaise and
Pink and White Pasta Shells
Simple Pink Salad Selection
Tuna Mousse

★★★★★★★★★★★

Pink Mashed Potato
Red Cabbage and Orange
Red Cabbage Salad
Pink Pasta Salad

★★★★★★★★★★★

Pink Apple Snow
Pink Meringues
White Meringues with Strawberry Cream
Strawberry Ice Cream with Pink Meringues
Vanilla and Raspberry Ice Cream Bombe
Rhubarb Fool
Raspberry or Strawberry Sorbet with Lemon
Sorbet

look as dainty as possible. Give little pink presents and prizes (a rubber, a tiny soap, etc.) and wrap these in pink tissue paper. When you serve the pudding put little bowls of mixed pink and white sugared almonds on the table, or pink and white peppermint stars (see page 123). Another idea is to give these as little presents. Put a few in some clingfilm and tie up as a little bundle, with pink parcel ribbon. Leave enough ribbon – about 3 inches (7.5 cm) for each strand – to make into curls (see page 13).

Green Party

As with the pink party, you may find it easier to make this party dual-colour for older children, to allow more flexibility re clothes, decorations and so on: it could be a green and white party, a green and yellow party, or green and red for Christmas.

Send out green invitation cards. You can buy bright emerald-green writing paper and envelopes which are sold loose, so that you don't have to buy more than you need. If you want to use a two-colour theme, have the envelope in one colour and the invitation in the other. The party-givers could cut the writing paper into half and send single sheet invitations decorated either by cutting the edges with pinking shears or putting fun green stickers on. Or fold the writing paper in half and send it as a stand-up card, shaped perhaps as an apple. If you want your guests to come in green clothes, or if you want to have a dual-colour theme (green and white or green and yellow), then state it here.

Decorate your party room with greenery from the garden, or if it is winter time use any green cactus or houseplants – green and cream poinsettia, for instance – to help carry the

---

MENU
GREEN PARTY

Spinach Soup with Tiny Croûtons
Watercress Soup
Avocado and Oranges with
Green Herb Dressing
Eggs with Green Mayonnaise or
Salad Cream
with
Brown Bread and Green Butter Pinwheels
Heart-Shaped Bread with Green Butter
Hot French Stick with Green Herb Butter
Rolls or French Stick with Green Butter

★★★★★★★★★★

Green Tagliatelli with Ham and
Chicken Cream Sauce
Spinach and Ham Pancakes
Cold Chicken with Watercress Sauce

★★★★★★★★★★

Green Salad
Broccoli, Peas, Beans, Spinach
New Potatoes with Chopped Parsley
Anna's Green Duchesse Potatoes

★★★★★★★★★★

Green or White Meringue with
Apple Cream Filling
Gooseberry Fool
Apple Sorbet
Green and White Fruit Salad

★★★★★★★★★★

Sage Derbyshire Cheese
Herb Roulé
Celery

theme through. Make green tissue flowers (see page 23). Put up green streamers (see page 14), green balloons, etc; carry on the theme with candles, napkins and, if you are planning to use them, paper plates. A friend who gave such a party placed on the centre of the table a bowl of green fruit, with Granny Smith apples, green grapes, greengages, green pears, etc, even including green bananas! After the meal offer little bowls of green and white peppermint creams (page 123.) If the children are still at an age for going-home presents then make them green and wrap them up in green tissue. Similarly if you are having games, try and find some suitably coloured prizes.

Try to prepare as much of the food in advance as possible (see pages 89–94), and don't worry if some of our suggestions seem a little outrageous: the children will love them!

Black and White Buffet Supper

We have included a black and white supper party for older children for a more sophisticated evening – possibly before going on to a black and white disco. Maybe you are planning to give one yourself. If you are, remember that probably not much will be eaten at a disco, so serve only finger food – dips, meringues, eclairs, black and white grapes, cherries, for instance. The quantities on page 95 are for eight; adapt the recipes to suit your numbers.

MENU
BLACK AND WHITE BUFFET

Curry or Horseradish Dip
with White Cauliflower Florets and
Mushroom Slices
Prunes Stuffed with Cream Cheese
Celery Sticks with Stilton and
Cream Cheese Filling
Black Grapes Stuffed with Cream Cheese
and Walnuts

★★★★★★★★★★

Chicken Salad with Black Grapes or
Cherries
Egg Salad with Mock Caviar
White Rice Salad with Raisins and Almond
Chinese Leaf Salad

★★★★★★★★★★

Lemon Syllabub with Black Cherries
Profiteroles (or Eclairs) and Chocolate Sauce
Chocolate Roulade
Yoghurt Cream Surprise
Blackcurrant/Blackberry Sorbet and Lemon
Sorbet

★★★★★★★★★★

Chèvre Blanc
Tomme aux Raisins
Rambol au Poivre
Brie

If your children would like to send out black invitations, you can now buy excellent silver pens which will show up on black card. As far as dress is concerned, while we appreciate that as children get older they are less likely to dress up, the sophistication of black and white seems to continue to appeal to the young.

Bare twigs can be painted with white emulsion. Leave some plain, or if they are not 'black' enough paint them with a black paint too. Alternatively do a zebra effect! Arrange these in pots in the party room to look like small trees (see page 14). If this is a party where you are giving out presents, wrap them in black and white paper and suspend them from the trees. Hang up black and white twisted streamers (see page 14). Black and white balloons (obtainable from party shops), and black and white candles will all help to create the right atmosphere.

As far as the food is concerned, the first section of the menu is for bits to serve with drinks; the second for the main-course buffet, and then just choose a couple of the black and white puds. However, this menu could also be adapted for a more formal sit-down dinner party.

Mixed Dinner Parties

We are only giving two alternative menus here as by this stage the young will know what they want to eat. These suggestions illustrate alternatives that can be easily prepared, are reasonably priced and are not difficult to serve up. For instance, consider whether you could make life easier by handing round individual ramekins rather than serving a large bowl of something. If the children are choosing alternative menus do remember various points:

1. Plan your menu so that the courses provide a variety of colours.
2. Make sure the textures are not all the same: for example don't start and finish with a mousse.
3. Don't repeat ingredients with, say, mushrooms in the starter, main dish and salad.
4. Always try and include something that is a little bit original. For example, if you want to give bread and butter, cut it out with a heart-shaped pastry cutter. It may be wasteful but it does look attractive (see page 100).

Perhaps the children could make the starter and/or the pudding and you the main course? Or you could simply do all the work together!

SUMMER MENU
MIXED DINNER PARTY

Chilled Cucumber Soup

★★★★★★★★★★★

Cherry Chicken Salad

★★★★★★★★★★★

Lemon Mousse or Fresh Fruit Salad (see pages 83 and 94)

WINTER MENU

Haddock Mousse with Heart-Shaped Bread and Butter

★★★★★★★★★★★

Lasagne and Salad
Baked Potatoes

★★★★★★★★★★★

Pavlova (see page 81) or Fruit Fondue

At the end why not serve Chocolate Truffles (see page 124) with the coffee, or iced coffee if it is summertime?

Match Parties

In this section, as well as suggestions for match teas or lunches and hints about organising your event, we have included a brief resumé of how to run various matches, such as football, cricket, rounders, tennis and a swimming gala! Everyone forgets! The matches can be shared between two or three families, which is fun, economical and less of a strain. All you need pray for is fine weather! (But if it does rain, see our Bad-Weather Contingency Plan on page 42).

Usually match parties take place away from your home. It is essential, therefore, that you make a list of everything you need to take with you. If you are feeding the children after the game, in the pavilion, then you will need to check what equipment is there: drying-up cloths, washing-up liquid, etc. Don't forget to take a dustbin liner with you for your rubbish.

Have enough helpers to allow you to leave everything neat and tidy. It may be the first time that a private party has been allowed to use the facilities, and it would be a shame to spoil opportunities for others by not having sufficient time to clear up properly. Also make sure you have enough transport available to ferry everyone and everything to and fro.

Depending on how elaborate a party you want, you could round the treat off by having a film show, barbecue, or perhaps a small disco. If you are embarking on these 'optional extras', then ensure that you have plenty of assistance.

Do remember to take a camera for a team photograph.

Football

First of all you will need to organise the venue. If you live in a town, why not ask your children's school whether or not it would be possible for you to hire their pitch? On the whole we have found people very encouraging to youngsters, and only too pleased to put themselves out to accommodate a game of this nature. If you are using a local pitch, you will have to choose a weekend when the team is not having a home match. Sometimes groundsmen will allow you to play on the morning of a match – but this would obviously depend on the state of the pitch and the attitude of the groundsman.

If your son is only nine or ten, playing on a full size pitch will be very tiring for him and his guests. Make allowances for this, by having half-time after twenty-five minutes instead of the usual forty-five, and perhaps inviting a few extra boys to fill up the pitch! It may also be a good idea to have two people in the goal mouths – these look huge with just one eight-year-old standing guard! Unless you have budding goalkeepers in your teams, you may well find this is not a popular place to fill when you come to select who plays where. By selecting *two* people for goal duty you may solve the problem.

Try to keep your teams even in their ability. If you are sharing the match with a friend who has invited the entire junior team of the local school, whilst your son's friends are less able, then try to be fair and have a flexible team-allocation system. We have found that organising the team placings in advance can avoid a complete walk-over by one or other of the teams and a lot of fuss at the time. It is important to keep the ages of your players as similar as possible – it is amazing how much a year's extra experience and strength makes at this stage.

You will need to have eleven players on each side but it is wise to have a couple of substitutes available in case anybody drops out at the last minute. An ideal way of getting round this is to choose, say, two younger brothers of team members who can, even if they do not play, have the responsibility of taking the oranges to the teams at half-time.

Tell your guests to come in whatever coloured strips your sons have chosen for the two teams. You will probably find that the colours will be determined by their favourite league team. T-shirts, sweatshirts, etc will be fine, so long as they are the right colour. Football boots should be worn for protection and to help stop slipping. If you can get hold of a qualified referee who will arrive in his black uniform then this adds prestige to the game. If not, don't forget a whistle. If you are really serious, employ a few fathers or brothers as linesmen (and don't forget a coin to toss with).

You will need to have about eight oranges, cut into segments with the skins on, for half-time refreshment. And as little prizes as they come off the pitch at the end of the match, why not give mini Mars bars to the winning team and Milky Way bars to the losers?

FOOTBALL MATCH FOOD

You will have to serve a lunch rather than a tea following your football match if the pitch is only available in the morning. If this is the case, you are going to be out for most of the morning and unless you can use any of the facilities that are near the pitch you must have everything prepared before you go. If twenty-two players are all descending on your house for lunch, then provide simple food, which you can leave cooking gently in the oven all morning. Just serve some ice cream and hot chocolate sauce for a pudding (see page 104 for recipes).

You will find that the children will be extremely thirsty, so give them all a squash-type drink as soon as they get in (have this prepared before you leave). You can then safely serve the fizzy drinks during the meal, but gulping the Coke on an empty stomach might prove unfortunate!

For starters, have $\frac{1}{2}$ gallon ($2\frac{1}{4}$ litres) of orange concentrate ready to mix up. For the meal they may get through eight large size ($3\frac{1}{2}$ pint/2 litre) bottles of Coke or lemonade.

After a drink they will be ravenous. Forget the dainty teas of tiny tots, they will be wanting something far more substantial. It is unlikely that they will have changed, so be prepared for them to be muddy, hot and hungry!

No doubt the team captains will have their own ideas as to what they want for their team lunch or team teas, so we are just giving you a few suggestions.

FOOTBALL TEAM LUNCHES

Oslo Steak Stew
Sausage Moussaka
Cheesy Meat and Potato Pie
Sausages

★★★★★★★★★★

Baked Potatoes
Quick Cooking Frozen Peas

★★★★★★★★★★

Ice Cream and Sauces

FOOTBALL TEAM TEAS

Sandwiches or soft rolls	1½ each

Fillings:
Sainsbury's soft pâté
Marmite and cucumber
Hard-boiled egg with salad cream
Ham and lettuce
Peanut butter
Cream cheese and chutney
Honey
Chocolate spread

Sausages	4 each
Bella's Cheese straws	2 each
Sausage Rolls	1 each
Cheese Scones	1 each
Biscuits	3 each

    Selection of bought biscuits
    Chocolate Shortbread Treat
    Shortbread Sandwich Biscuits
    Chocolate Crunch Cakes
    Meringues (see page 88)
    Nutty Chocolate Treat
    Cornflake/Ricicle Specials
    Quick and Easy Fabulous Flapjacks
    Peanut Cookies

Cakes	1 piece each

    Iced Cup Cakes
    Praline Cake
    Match Cake

Cricket

If your son is a keen cricketer, you could share a match with another friend. However, you might find it quite hard to muster eleven for each side during the summer holidays when friends are away. Make sure that you have a sufficiently long list of possible players before you actually book anything. The next problem is finding a local pitch available for a suitable date. It is probably best to choose a weekend as you will need help from the dads for this match. You must have two competent scorers so that one can have a break, and at least two umpires. (It is preferable to have four people available to umpire so that *if* it is a very hot day they can have a break after the first innings.)

As far as equipment goes you will need to provide the ball, two bats, two pairs of pads, two pairs of gloves, plus a pair of pads and gloves for a wicket keeper, two sets of stumps and bails and a score sheet, not to mention the coin to make the toss with! Most boys who are keen on cricket seem to have their own equipment, but it is probably sensible if between the two teams you have the basic essentials supplied. As the boys get older they really should wear cricket boots so that they have more protection and do not slip. If they do not have these then it's a good idea to suggest that trainers rather than tennis shoes be worn.

You will have your own ideas as to how the match should be run, but do try to make sure your teams are as evenly matched as possible – it will result in a much better game. In our experience we have found it best if everybody has an opportunity to bat. Either arrange for each boy to have a certain number of overs, or to retire once they have made, say, twenty runs. You may feel it is not such a good idea to have everybody bowling – a feeble over might give the opposing team too much of an advantage.

It is a good idea to run this sort of match according to a time schedule, so if you start at 2 pm, have tea at 4 pm, and end the match at 6 pm. If the teams are ill-matched and you find it is a complete walkover for one team, then have a second match with rearranged teams. Another idea if the match is over too early is to play tip and run, where if you hit the ball with the bat you have to run no matter what.

Remind both captains before the match that it is very boring fielding all afternoon on the boundary. Try to ensure that every boy who has not bowled feels that he has played a part in the match by, for example, fielding near the wicket.

CRICKET TEAS

You may find that the mid-match tea is not devoured as hastily as you expected. The adrenalin is still flowing and match nerves can take away some boys' appetites. However, you will need plenty of drink, especially if the weather is hot. Then if you leave the teatime leftovers out in clingfilm, you will find that they will disappear rapidly once the match has finished.

Don't forget that you will need to feed and water the helpers, and you may well find that several of the parents will stay and watch the match. Provide enough tea for everybody to tuck into! No doubt your child will have his or her own ideas as to what they want for the team tea, but look at some of our suggestions on page 105. Make a cricket pitch match cake if it is a birthday celebration.

Drink. You will need a lot of drink throughout the afternoon, so have plenty available. We suggest half a dozen of the largest $3\frac{1}{2}$ pint (2 litre) bottles of Coke or lemonade; a $\frac{1}{2}$ gallon (2.25 litres) of orange concentrate ready to mix up; and lemon concentrate (you could mix the lemon and orange as it makes a very refreshing drink). If you have a suitable container then freeze bags of ice prior to your match day and, keeping it in the cold box, put some into each jug as you make it up.

Rounders

Anyone, whether sporty or not, can enjoy a game of rounders. You really need nine players a side, but if you have either less or more that is no problem at all. In fact, this is what makes rounders such an ideal party game. It can have a flexible number of participants, and you use very little equipment.

Players, divided into two teams, will include a bowler, backstop (a kind of wicket-keeper to stand behind the batsman), four 'posts' who are fielders, and three outfielders or deep fielders. Additional team members can be extra outside fielders, standing behind and between the posts. The posts must not hinder the batsmen as they run. The four posts are marked by objects such as paint cans, bean poles, or whatever you have to hand. The batsman uses either a proper rounders bat, a cricket bat, a tennis racket (the only problem here is that a tennis racket can hit the ball far too far), or simply the batsman's hand. The ball can be a proper hard rounders ball if playing with a bat, or use just a tennis ball (particularly if you are using hands to hit it with!).

In case you have forgotten how to play rounders, here is a brief rundown of the rules. The batsman tries to hit the ball, but if he misses he can still run to the first post. If he

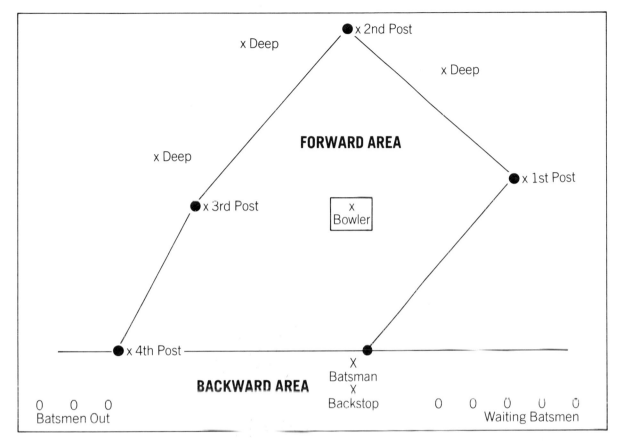

x 2nd Post

x Deep

x Deep

FORWARD AREA

x Deep

x 1st Post

x 3rd Post

x
Bowler

x 4th Post

BACKWARD AREA

X
Batsman
X
Backstop

0   0   0
Batsmen Out

0   0   0   0   0
Waiting Batsmen

does hit the ball he can try to score a rounder by running round all four posts, while the other side tries to get him out by stumping him with the ball. If you haven't played rounders you can easily get hold of a copy of the rules from a library. If you don't actually have anyone scoring the number of rounders made, then make sure that the team captains remember to make a tally.

The match (playing time) will be an hour if you allow fifteen minutes per innings, and give each team two innings. Have a little practice time if you have guests who have not played before. Take some squash and biscuits for a half-time break. Remind guests to come with a sweater or sweatshirt in case of need.

Tennis

TENNIS PARTY FOR SIX CHILDREN

If you want to organise a tennis party do wait until children are experienced enough to play the game at least moderately well! If you book one court for the six children, the actual tennis will take almost $2\frac{1}{2}$ hours to play. Don't be put off by this, because it will be organised so that every child plays every other child (each playing five matches).

As usual, the secret of success is to organise everything efficiently beforehand, and you should make a match chart (see page 33). Each match will consist of three games and the number of games won goes on the chart. To discover the overall winner you simply add together the number of games won: whoever has achieved most wins is the *victor ludorum*. We suggest you award six prizes: a first, second and third graduated prizes, and then three identical smaller prizes to those left. In this way it is not so obvious who achieved least.

Whilst a game is going on, there will be four children left over, two of whom can ball-boy. The other two can sit on a ground sheet watching the match, with puzzles and cards, etc, available to play with if they wish. It will work out that sometimes a child will have to go from playing to being a ball-boy instead of having a rest, but everyone will be able to sit down at some point. It is a good idea to play tennis for $1\frac{1}{4}$ hours, say, and then have a complete break. Your timetable might be as follows:

Everyone comes at 3 pm, and you give them a biscuit or piece of cake and a drink, followed by tennis for $1\frac{1}{4}$–$1\frac{1}{2}$ hours. Then have a break for about 15 minutes doing something totally different, and again have something small to eat. An inventive friend who had a tennis party at her home hung doughnuts on string from her whirlygig washing line, which amalgamated something to eat, a fun game *and* a break from

The timetable would look like this:	
3.00 Arrive	**6.30** End games
3.15 Tea (light)	**7.00** Barbecue
3.45 Tennis starts	**7.45** Games
5.00 Refreshments	**8.30** Go home
5.15 Tennis	

the tennis! Have plenty of soft drinks available all the time, as everyone including yourself will probably be very thirsty. You then continue the tennis for about another $1\frac{1}{4}$ hours. Afterwards, perhaps have a simple barbecue supper.

We suggest that you umpire for the younger age group (take a light folding chair). For a tournament for six children you will need to have fifteen match score sheets, plus the final score chart and a pencil or pen. Remember how easy it is to forget the score even when you are playing. It is even easier to lose count if one of the other guests asks a question which distracts you for a moment. So be prepared and mark a simple score sheet (see below) with dots as points are won. Put the servers on the top row each time.

If the weather is cold but still fine, check that everybody has some warm clothing to put on while they are not playing (remember

SCORE SHEET	HOLLY v REBECCA															
---	---	---	---	---	---	---	---	---	---	---	---	---	---	---	Rebecca	Holly
SERVER															Rebecca	Holly
Rebecca	●	●	●				●		●	●					1	
				●	●	●		●								
Holly		●	●		●	●										1
	●			●												
Rebecca		●	●													
	●			●	●	●										1

Individual Match Scores								

Individual Match Scores

1.	Julia	0	**2.**	Susan	0	**3.**	Holly	3
	Michelle	3		Rebecca	3		Kirsty	0
4.	Julia	2	**5.**	Michelle	1	**6.**	Susan	3
	Susan	1		Holly	2		Kirsty	0
7.	Julia	2	**8.**	Kirsty	0	**9.**	Holly	2
	Rebecca	1		Michelle	3		Susan	1
10.	Julia	3	**11.**	Michelle	1	**12.**	Rebecca	3
	Kirsty	0		Susan	2		Kirsty	0
13.	Julia	3	**14.**	Rebecca	0	**15.**	Holly	2
	Holly	0		Michelle	3		Rebecca	1

FINAL SCORES

	games won	matches won	Place
JULIA	10	4	2nd
HOLLY	9	4	3rd
SUSAN	7	2	5th
KIRSTY	0	0	6th
REBECCA	8	2	4th
MICHELLE	11	3	1st

something for yourself as well). If the weather is so appalling that you can't play, have a contingency plan already worked out.

LARGE MIXED DOUBLES TENNIS PARTY

The key to the number of people to invite lies in the number of tennis courts you can use, and the length of time for which they will be available. Remember that children will be slower than adults playing their games: for example, their serving takes much longer, and an average set will last about 25 minutes. The number invited must be divisible by four. Twelve or sixteen are ideal numbers. You could manage with twelve on one court, but it would take the whole afternoon. Sixteen to twenty people on two courts, and twenty-four to twenty-eight on three courts works well.

If you run the party from, say, 10 am to 4 pm you can give guests individual picnic lunches (see page 51) which they can eat at whatever time they choose, rather than have everybody stopping for a meal which takes up valuable time. The way this party is devised allows everybody to play with everybody else, until after a certain length of time players may start playing with somebody they have already played with.

Here is a list of things you will require:

1. Some other activity to keep people occupied when they are not playing: swing ball, table tennis (if at home), etc, or organise an extra court for practising. If facilities are limited, take plenty of electronic games.

2. Score sheet and chart, see below.
3. A red and blue pen, and a pencil – *very important*. Blackboard stand and boards, if possible. If not, hardboard to pin charts to.
4. Plenty of soft drinks. Collect large plastic bottles in advance of the event and fill with diluted squash, and take yoghurt pots or similar for glasses. It is also a good idea to have some biscuits as well as the picnic.
5. Prizes.
6. Plenty of tennis balls.
7. Remind everyone to bring warm clothing for when they are not playing.
8. The picnic itself. See pages 51–52 for suggestions.

With younger children we suggest you play five games for one match, changing ends after the first game, and thereafter after every two games (someone gets two serves). If the children are playing very good tennis, you may want to play a complete set for a winner.

Our tournament structure may seem complicated, but it works extremely well and is very fair. Usually the problem with running a doubles tournament is that people can get stuck with one player for the morning and one for the afternoon, and this can cause a very unfair result at the end of the day. By this method the players change partners every match, with a boy always playing with a girl, and this has the added advantage that the children all meet and mix with each other.

Study the chart carefully. In the winning

TOURNAMENT CHART			TO BE COMPLETED BY ADULT	
Round 1	Round 2	Round 3	Round 4	Round 5
3 Edward/Camilla v Nicholas/Clare 2	4 Nicholas/Alison v James/Clare 1	James/Lucy v Sam/Clare		
1 Sam/Kate v James/Jane 4	3 Sam/Camilla v Charles/Kate 2	Charles/Alison v Jonathan/Kate		
2 John/Susan v Charles/Julia 3	5 Jonathan/Susan v John/Jane 0	John/Camilla v Edward/Jane		
5 Jonathan/Alison v Tom/Lucy 0	1 Tom/Julia v Edward/Lucy 4	Tom/Susan v Nicholas/Julia		
WINNING BOY MOVES UP WINNING GIRL MOVES DOWN Losers stay same level but play each other				

A sparkling disco party (see page 8).

Fun on the football pitch (see page 27).

SCORE SHEET

Children complete this sheet themselves

Name	Round 1	Round 2	Round 3	Round 4	Round 5	Round 6
Edward	3	4				
Nicholas	2	4				
Sam	1	3				
James	4	1				
John	2	0				
Charles	3	2				
Jonathan	5	5				
Tom	0	1				

	Round 1	Round 2	Round 3	Round 4	Round 5	Round 6
Camilla	3	3				
Clare	2	1				
Kate	1	2				
Susan	4	0				
Julia	2	5				
Alison	3	1				
Lucy	5	4				
Jane	0	4				

partnership, the boy always moves up a game, the winning girl always moves down a game. The losing boy and girl partnership then move across on the same level, but are playing opposite each other.

Always fill in the losing pairs' next round position first – this is *very important*. It also helps to underline the boys' names in red, the girls' in blue. Pin the chart to the board. When each game finishes the children come and tell the adult in charge of the chart the score. The adult must then move the children to their next appropriate game, and fill in the next round on the chart.

On the other side of the board will be the sheet on which the children record their own scores – simply the number of games they have won with their partner. During the match the children will score for themselves. Have one person by the blackboard at all times, just checking that the information put down is correct!

Swimming

If you are lucky enough to have your own swimming pool make the most of it and have a swimming gala and a barbecue. Otherwise try and borrow your school's pool or see if your local pool could be available. Do make sure the swimming pool is warm enough for this particular occasion – your family may be used to it freezing cold, but it is so much more pleasant if you have it around 80°F (27°C) just this once!

Really you need not organise too many games as the children will enjoy themselves anyway. Bear in mind that some children will not be experienced swimmers and may not be confident in the water: watch out for this, and encourage them. If some cannot dive, let them start in the water for races. Say that if there is anyone who does not like diving they must get into the water first (although children hate saying they cannot do things). If you find that someone turns out to be a complete beginner let them splash around at the shallow end when everyone is mucking about, but once the races begin whisk them out and ask them to help you organise the games – without giving them any option!

The timing of the party rather depends on when you want to feed the children. If you want to do a barbecue lunch, then you might prefer to have the swimming in the morning, rather than waiting for half an hour until their food is digested and they are able to swim.

Otherwise have them arrive mid-afternoon and prepare a barbecue high tea or supper, depending on their ages (the barbecue recipes are for eight, so adapt to fit your numbers).

Don't invite too many children – that is when accidents happen. Always have an adult in swimming things in attendance, doing nothing else but keeping an eye on the children from the safety point of view – not organising games. Make sure someone knows mouth-to-mouth resuscitation. Tell the children not to run around the sides: it is all too easy for accidents to happen when there are a lot of children getting in and out of the water and making the edge of the pool wet and slippery.

Below are a few suggestions for games and races to play in the pool if there's room.

SIMPLE STROKE RACES
Crawl, backstroke, breaststroke, relay-team race, etc.

NOVELTY HAT RACE
Provide a funny hat – nothing precious – for each team. The race will start and the hand-overs will take place in the water.

MUSICAL BALLOONS
This is the same idea as musical chairs, but if it is a windy day you will have to use balls (that can't be blown out of the pool) instead of balloons. When the music stops everybody has to swim for a balloon and if they don't get one then they are out. Remove one balloon each round. Whoever grabs the last balloon is the winner.

HOT POTATO GAME
The children all swim around with the music playing. One child has a ball which they throw to a neighbour, shouting out their name. Whoever is named has to pick up the ball and throw it on to somebody else. Whoever has the ball when the music stops is out.

BALLOON RACE

The children must swim a length with the balloon in their mouth and hand the balloon to the next person in their team, who repeats the performance. When the last member of the team finishes, the balloon has to be burst before the race is won.

OVER AND UNDER RACE

This is really only suitable for older children to play. One member of the team jumps in the pool and the next one follows him and swims between his legs to take up a position just beyond him. The third member of the team jumps in, goes through the legs of the first one, and then has to swim over the top of the second one who goes down in the water. They then stand in their position with their legs open for the fourth person, who jumps in the pool through the legs, over the next, through the legs again and is ready and waiting for the next person to go over the top. It rather depends on the depth of the pool as to how long this race can go on for. If necessary, divide the teams into small numbers and either go across the pool widthwise or, if the children are large enough, do it going towards the deeper end. In either case, you will probably need to run hoats.

FOLLOW MY LEADER

This is not a race, just a game where the children have to do whatever a 'leader' does. Get various children to have a go as the leader, but don't allow them to run in and out of the pool in case of accidents

READY STEADY AND ALL GO

You will probably have to do this race as a timed heat, with each team swimming individually. The fastest team is the winner. The number in each team would be dependent on the width of the pool. The children stand in a line holding hands and jump in at the deep end. They then have to swim the length of the pool, holding hands all the time. When they get to the shallow end they have to clamber out, still holding hands. The children at either end can obviously help most because they·have one hand free.

HELPFUL HINTS

1. Twenty children would be enough for this kind of party. And for that you would need four adults to help organise, one of whom must be there simply to be ready to jump in if necessary.

2. Depending on the age of the children, the actual swimming time should not be more than two hours. If you are thinking of making it an evening party, remember that even in the height of summer it will be cool for the children.

3. Check before everybody (the 'lifeguard' too) goes in the pool that they are not wearing watches, unless they are waterproof.

4. If you are giving a single-sex party in a private pool and do not have a changing room outside, place some chairs in a corner of the garden where the children could change to avoid twenty pairs of wet feet paddling through the house.

5. Tell the children to keep their towels nearby as they will need them while they are standing about – if they are out of a game, or while the rest of their team are swimming.

6. Plan the barbecue timing carefully.

7. Have some games planned – not too active! to play when the children have finished their meal.

8. If you want to show a video film after the party instead of playing games this can be a useful in-built contingency plan in case the weather changes.

Lunch and Activity Parties

There comes a time, around eight years old, when children have grown out of the conventional tea party, but are still too young to play matches. They are at an age when they will enjoy an outdoor 'fun-day' party. They can ask as many as your garden – and you – can cope with! Invite guests for a lunch and arrange to have a Dad around to help organise and control. You will certainly need some helpers anyway. Depending on the weather, you can get the children out of the house and doing something active to work off a bit of steam. Have the party from 12.30 to 3 pm which will give you half an hour of activity before lunch at about 1, and probably an hour and a half of activity following lunch – which disappears amazingly quickly!

Food

As far as the food goes, if the weather is good, provide a barbecue (see pages 67–73). If not, it is best to keep everything simple. We have included a few ideas to make conventional menus a bit different (see pages 110–111). Don't bother with a starter, but always cook some sausages (allow two per person); if there are children who don't like their main course, then you have a pretty safe alternative to offer them (and you can serve a sausage each,

anyway, with any of these main courses). The recipes are for eight so adjust them to suit your numbers.

Arrange to have someone organising arrival games so that you can be putting final touches to lunch. It is so much easier to be thoroughly organised beforehand and to keep everything very uncomplicated – all our suggestions are deliberately so!

MENU I

Barbecue (see pages 67–73)

★★★★★★★★★★

Ice Cream with Butterscotch Sauce (see page 104)
Bananas au Chocolat (see page 73)

MENU II

Home-made Beefburgers
Devilled Chicken Drumsticks (hot or cold)
Bacon Jacket Potatoes
Sausage Moussaka (see page 103)
Pigs in a Blanket
Bowls of Tomato Sauce

★★★★★★★★★★

Plum and Apple Crumble with Vanilla Ice Cream
Lemon Pudding
Chocolate Mallows

Assault Course

If the weather is being kind, younger children will relish the challenge that an assault course brings. Let them divide into teams, or give individuals a time score – the *victor ludorum* will be the one with the fastest time (you will need a stopwatch for this). Organise a practice run before lunch, and afterwards allow a suitable length of time to allow their meal to go down. (Play a quieter game in this period – a garden treasure hunt, for instance, see page 42.) Be prepared for English weather to ruin your ideas and have a contingency plan to turn to in case of need (see page 42).

We found that a points system worked the best, so that if you win you earn five points, and losers still score some points, say two. Hopefully this will avoid the losing team becoming very disheartened. Have a scoreboard of some sort to keep the tally. Use either a washing line lying straight on the ground or bean poles to mark the start and finish. The size of your garden and the type of equipment you have to hand will dictate what sort of course you wish to run. Once the children have used an item – the egg and spoon, say – either make them take the articles back for the next person before they move on to the next obstacle, or have them doing so in a reverse form on the way to the finish. Alternatively, have enough helpers to organise this for the children.

POSSIBLE OBSTACLES

Always organise your props well ahead.

1. Going through a tyre (hanging up or on ground), or through an open ended barrel.

2. Dressing up – huge wellingtons, skirt and hat.

3. Running in a sack (dustbin liner will do).

4. Throwing a ball into a bucket. If the children are older you could substitute with a pitch and putt alternative.

5. Egg and spoon (use potatoes).

6. Stepping stones (use concrete blocks or whatever you have to hand, but if the children are getting older why not make them go backwards over these?). Or run along a board balanced on two tyres or straw bales.

7. Bending in between bean poles, kicking a football, and then shooting at a 'goal' – two bean poles making each goal.

8. Picking up six Smarties with a straw and dropping them into a bowl.

9. Bobbing for an apple.

10. Climbing a rope ladder, and touching a certain point.

11. Long jump or high jump.

12. Running on stilts. You can buy mini-stilts or make them from two identical cocoa-cans or similar (do not use cans opened by a can opener because of the sharp edges). Thread a thin piece of string or washing line, about 4 ft (120 cm) long, through two holes on either side of the can. The children balance on the cans and use the loop as the stilt.

13. Throwing a wellington into a hoop which is lying on the ground.

14. A somersault over the finish line. If a relay race, when one team member has completed the requisite number of obstacles, the next member then sets off. The individual's time can be recorded, and the victor is the one who is the fastest.

Bike Gymkhana

If you have a suitable garden or access to a nearby flat open space, you can hold a bike gymkhana. (Don't let them ride on soggy grass, however, as it could mean a wrecked lawn!) You can either ask your guests to come equipped with their own bikes, depending on the numbers involved and the space you have, or run two teams and just have two bicycles which everyone uses. This saves problems of transporting bikes any distance. If everyone brings a bike, include a fancy-dress class. Everyone arrives togged up and the fancy dress is judged before lunch. All can be normal then for the serious stuff of racing after the meal. You need not have races all the time, and you can play other games (see page 41) as well, but make the theme of the party the bicycle 'bit'.

If your guests all bring bikes, you can have race heats and then a final, depending on numbers. In either event, team or individual racing, keep a scoreboard and record points for winning, coming second, etc. The ultimate overall winner will have most points at the end of the day. You should be in charge of the scoreboard – pin up a large piece of paper on which to write the points. Have this organised well in advance, and have some little prizes ready.

Remember you will have plenty of props to organise. If you have to go to an open space, pack the car in advance ready to go straight after lunch. Have a checklist of props! Even if you are at home, be well prepared before everyone arrives. The following are a few ideas for games.

BENDING RACE
Place bending (bean) poles between which the riders have to go. It can either be the fastest rider who wins or the slowest, or do both – but separately of course!

COLLECTING THE CAN
Place empty yoghurt pots or similar on top of each of the bean poles. Place a bucket by each 'start'. The riders have to collect the pots off the bean poles and bring them back to the bucket one by one. If doing this as a team race, have the next member taking the pots back one by one and replacing them, and carry on in this way, turn and turn about.

OBSTACLE RACE
The rider bikes to a point where he has to get off and put on a hat and scarf and gloves. He gets back on and goes on to the next point where he has to bike round a circle of bricks which are laid on the ground. He bikes back, takes off his hat, gloves and scarf, and then bikes back to the start.

APPLE BOBBING
Bike to a bowl with water and apples in and bob one out. Race back to the start.

SPEEDWAY
Whoever is fastest wins!

SLOW BICYCLE RACE
Whoever is the slowest wins.

Hiring a Bouncy Castle

Children seem to adore bouncy castles – you will have seen them at local events. We have an amazing friend who hired one privately for her daughter's party, and it was the greatest success. Shop around and ask about hiring if you see one being used anywhere – a local council, a zoo or safari park or even Yellow Pages might be able to help. The charge is quite high, but comparable to hiring an entertainer or magician.

Obviously this is for a fine weather party, and you will need to have sufficient space in your garden to accommodate the castle. They come in various sizes, but if you can't find a small one, ask your school if you could hire their playing field. Share the cost and the party with a friend, then you could give a picnic tea and have additional outdoor games on the field.

NB: Children are not allowed to wear shoes when bouncing.

Outdoor Games

This is a selection of outdoor games which you can include with any outside party.

THROWING THE WELLIE
You need a lot of space for this game. Have a number of old tyres or hoops and number these 10, 4, 2, etc. The children throw the wellies from a starting line into the tyres or hoops. Whoever has the highest score wins. Have a score sheet.

MATCHBOX HUNT
Let the children either play in pairs or as individuals. Give each child, or pair, a matchbox. Tell them to find as many different things as they can fit into the matchbox in two minutes. Whoever collects most is the winner.

PITCH AND PUTT
This is a surprisingly difficult game. You will need golf balls and suitable clubs; targets and their score markers – old bamboo sticks slit with paper markers; score sheet and pencils; washing line for base line; short grass (that's not too precious!).

Allow two children to have their turns together (or play as a team game). The children stand behind a line and chip golf balls into the following: a tyre, box, paddling pool, or a circle painted on the ground. Don't put these too far away. Each target must have a score marker by it, with different scores. Whoever gets the highest score wins. Allow one or two shots at each target. Children retrieve their balls after their turn and the next guest has a try.

SHIPWRECK
Choose a child to be 'He'. The 'He' chases the other children who are only safe when off the ground, on straw bales, rugs, newspapers, etc, which serve as islands. If a child is touched by the 'He' while not on an island, then that guest takes over and chases the others. There is no real winner to this game: it can go on until you think the children have had enough.

SACK RACE
Have one sack per guest or use only two sacks and divide the guests into two teams, making it into a team sack race. If real sacks cannot be found, use dustbin liners (but they're not so durable).

WHEELBARROW RACE
Play this game before tea, or not until well after tea. Again pair the children off. One acts as the wheelbarrow, walking on his or her hands, and one as the 'pusher', holding the 'wheelbarrow's' legs.

THREE-LEGGED RACE

Have plenty of large men's handkerchiefs or dusters, and pair the children off. Tie their inside legs together.

BALLOON RACE

You will need two balloons per child or per team, plus two elastic bands (buy *more* than you need). Slip an elastic band securely round the knot of the balloon so it forms a loop. Children attach a balloon to each ankle with the elastic band. When the whistle blows they race to the winning line – without falling over or bursting their balloons.

GARDEN HUNT

You will need pieces of wool, card etc. This is an outdoor version of the Treasure Hunt (see page 62). Prepare and play it in the same way, the only difference being that, because you're out of doors, you should make sure that the clue cards won't blow away by firmly securing them (to a branch, under a pot, etc). Instead of numbered cards, you could use a length of different coloured thread, wool or string (red for the first clue, blue for the second and so on), which the children bring back to you. Suggestions for clues depend on ages.

Simple ones might be:

Around garden tap	Under greenhouse
Under bucket	door
Beside bicycle	Under stone
Under flower pot	Under garden seat
On branch of tree	Beside steps

FRENCH CRICKET

You will need a tennis ball and some sort of bat. There is no winner with this game, but children enjoy playing it. Someone stands with either a tennis racket or a cricket bat. Using a tennis ball the other children try to get the batsman out, by hitting his legs below the knees. If the batsman hits the ball he can turn to face the way the ball will be coming back at him. If however he has missed it, he is not allowed to do this, and must keep his feet in the same position (awkward when the ball is being bowled from behind him!).

Bad-Weather Contingency Plans

When you plan an outdoor party of any sort, always have a contingency plan up your sleeve in case the weather lets you down. Don't leave it until the day dawns wet and windy before you decide what to do. Be prepared and it will never happen! Check for example what films are on locally, and the times of performances, or take the children to the nearest sports hall or ice rink. Do your research thoroughly: can you bring food along and eat indoors wherever you are going, for instance, or would it be better to have your food at home? Think about the costs involved, and the transport you will require. Or you may prefer to entertain your guests at home. Look at the indoor games suggested (see page 61). But in any case have your plans formulated well before the day itself.

Another idea might be to run an indoor Olympics. You would need to have organised things prior to the event, and you may need to borrow some games from friends. Operate a points decision – remember to give the losers a few points as well after each contest so that everybody has some score. You can make this a team event, or pair your guests off, or allow the individuals to compete for themselves. The type of games you play will largely be dictated by the size of your house. If it is possible to have some sort of game per pair of guests then everybody should be occupied at least to begin with. Some games will take longer than others to complete, and you should have time limits for longer ones so that everybody has a shot at all of them.

Here is a list of ideas from which to choose: mini-snooker; table tennis; electronic games; television games; cards (Snap, Beggar My Neighbour, etc); board games (put on time limits); Subbuteo or similar; Scalextrix or similar.

You will need:

1. Sufficient adults to help organise the score sheet and to referee the games.
2. To have checked that you have no dud batteries in the games.
3. Sufficient table tennis balls to allow for breakages.
4. To try to avoid games which you know will take a very long time to complete (Monopoly, for instance).
5. To draw up a points table, listing your guests' names, and with headings of the games you decide to play. There will be no ruffled feathers at the end of the day as the points earned will show clearly and will be indisputable!

Presents and Prizes

You will still be requiring presents and prizes for younger age-group parties – the older ones will not need them – and we suggest that you ask your children to help you choose the little goodies. Last year's fashions will be dated this year so you'll have to be guided. But be warned – the smaller the gift, often the more expensive it is!

If you are giving out prizes for games throughout the party, it is a good idea to provide each guest with a little bag to put them into. You can write each child's name on an ordinary paper bag, or carry on your party theme: decorate a piece of card with a bicycle, for a bike gymkhana, print the child's name on it, and staple it to a bag. Some party shops actually sell suitable bags marked 'loot', which are great fun, but obviously the cost quickly mounts up!

Bought presents can include items like:

Pencil sharpeners
Little pencils and notebooks
Small packets of sweets, Smarties, etc.
Mini soaps
Fun stickers
Little selections of sweets (put a few different sweets in pieces of clingfilm, twist the top of the film and tie with a pretty ribbon)
Jokes and nasties (trick fly, trick sugar lumps, etc.)
Fun-shaped rubbers
Coloured marker pens

However, if you want to save the pennies and give home-made sweets as presents, we give some ideas on page 122.

Outings and Picnic Parties

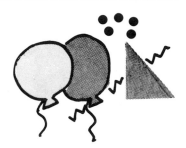

First of all, discuss with your children where they would like to go. We and our friends have visited swimming and wave-machine pools, ice- and roller-skating rinks, been to a football match and horse events, and taken groups to a leisure centre, cinemas and the theatre. For an outing that couldn't be nearer or cheaper, but is still extremely popular, try camping out in the garden (after a barbecue supper).

If you have just arrived in your area, or simply want to find somewhere new to take the children, make use of your local museum or library. They both have a fund of information which they are only too glad to share. They will provide an exhaustive list of local galleries, country houses, castles, mills, forts, nature reserves, country and wild-life parks: even if you think you know your part of the world well we're sure you'll find that you haven't been to half of them!

Check out exactly what you are letting yourself in for well in advance, by either writing for a brochure or maybe even doing a recce first. Check the opening and closing times, and that wherever you are going is open on the particular day you have chosen. Check your costings and what extra costs you may incur when you get there. Plan to play a few games in the car (see page 52) and have a couple of outdoor games organised to fill in any gaps when you arrive at your destination.

We have included plenty of advice about picnics if you wish to provide the food yourself. However, if you are travelling far, and the weather might be a problem, we suggest that you stop at a restaurant chain – which the children will love even if you don't! – and they are quite reasonably priced.

When organising an outing, invite your guests half an hour earlier than the time you plan to leave. This allows for the one who is going to be late! If your outing is to be an all-day affair – and you don't want to have the aggravation of being back at a certain time – either arrange to drop everyone off at their homes, or invite guests to stay for an early supper, or even the night. Remember, though, that it will be an exhausting day for *you* before you commit yourself to too much! Always take a telephone number of one parent who could let the others know if you are going to be delayed.

Be well organised in advance, and you will be less likely to leave the picnic food or anything else behind. Have a checklist – and remember to check it. If you have large numbers of children to cope with, take a checklist of the children's names and do occasional head counts throughout the day! Only ask numbers that can be seated comfortably in the car – or cars, as it is a very good idea to organise a party with a friend so that you can take *two* cars. It is much better to ask fewer guests than have an uncomfortable journey; even if you have an estate car, don't think of it as a mini-bus! (You could hire a mini-bus, but that is an expensive exercise.) Don't plan to go too far – it will be a tiring day. Always have a contingency plan ready if the weather is really unpleasant (see pages 42–43). Whatever the weather, you should ask your guests to bring a waterproof of some sort with them. Most important of all, choose a meeting place or instruct children to find a policeman if anyone gets separated.

If you want, you can plan a surprise party and devise a mystery outing, not telling the children where they will be going.

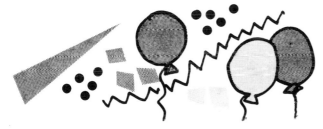

Swimming Pool or Wave-Machine Pool

There are no two ways about it, taking a group of children to a swimming pool is a great responsibility. When you visit a wave-machine pool, you must remember that the wave created is quite strong, so do make sure that all your guests really can swim. Unless you really have a lot of helpers, try not to take children under the age of nine.

Always have helpers – one helper to four children, depending on the children's age and ability. A friend who organised this treat for her daughter tied markers of ribbon on the girls' swimming-costume shoulder straps. She imagined that this would make it easier for her to keep an eye on her 'brood'. However, in the mêlée of children in the pool there was no way that these properly singled out her group. What we are saying is that it is going to be difficult for you to have your eyes everywhere, and you don't want to be too restrictive in what you tell the children they can or cannot do or you will spoil the party. Perhaps a good hint is to find out from your local pool which is their quietest day, and plan your treat around that.

Remember that you may need change for locker keys in the changing rooms, so check that at the same time. When you organise the event, stress that no watches nor jewellery should be brought. We would also suggest that you put a dustbin liner in the car so that all the wet things can be put into it.

Even if *you* do not feel like swimming, it is a good idea for you – or your helpers – to be in a swimming costume in case you have to jump in quickly.

Scheduling really depends how long a day you want to make this treat. You could go to the wave-machine pool in the morning and come back for lunch, in which case you would probably ask everyone to be at your house at around 9.30 am and be collected at 2 pm. Or you could have a lunch at home with everybody coming at about 12 pm, then take them to the pool (allow half an hour after eating before they swim) and give them a picnic or hot snack afterwards, in which case they would be picked up at about 6 pm. Don't forget that whenever you go, the children will be extremely hungry immediately after their swimming, so either be prepared to fork out and buy something at the pool, or take some goodies with you.

If you want to find out if there is a wave

machine pool near you, look in the Yellow Pages under swimming pools and public baths. Your local pool will tell you if they know of one nearby. Check opening times before fixing the time of the party.

Ice Skating

At the moment, ice-skating rinks are few and far between. Check in the Yellow Pages or ask at your local library or town hall to see if there is one in your area. Organise this do with a friend and, depending on the numbers involved, take two cars.

Make sure you know the way to the rink; most provide a brochure with instructions, if requested. It is best to go at the quietest time of day if you are taking a group of children, particularly if some of them have not skated before. Telephone the rink when you are first planning the outing and you will find them very helpful. If you want coaching for the children this could be arranged at the same time. If the children are beginners, then tell them to come with gloves, and the girls to wear jeans not skirts. This is to protect them if (or when) they fall over.

When you arrive at the rink the children may have to queue for their skates and similarly at the end for their shoes. This can take quite a time, so allow for it in your calculations if you want to get off home promptly. When the children ask for their skates they have to give their shoe size. It is important that you check that their laces are done up sufficiently tightly, particularly around the ankles. Indeed, you may find yourself doing up everybody's skates for them. If you are not skating yourself, go with warm clothes – it is a bit chilly! You can sit by the side of the rink and keep an eye on everybody – and buy hot drinks to warm

yourself up. A friend will give you an extra pair of hands if there is any problem, either on or off the ice. Having experienced this, we know it *can* happen!

When the children have finished skating they will be thirsty and probably peckish. If you don't want to spend more money buying refreshments, take a basket of sustenance with you in the car (biscuits, crisps and drink).

If you were planning this activity as a birthday treat for an under-twelve, and if it involves a long motorway drive, it might be worthwhile contacting a quick food restaurant en route and asking them to organise a birthday meal for you. Happy Eater, Pizzaland and Little Chef will organise parties if they have sufficient warning.

Roller Skating

Roller-skating rinks are also few and far between, so you may find yourself driving miles. Once again, we suggest that you organise this event with a friend. As many children can roller skate at home, try to take a group who are roughly the same standard. Otherwise, the ones who cannot skate will probably feel rather left out.

You can hire or use your own skates. Telephone the rink and check which times would be the best for your group: you will find, for instance, that there are disco periods when the skating can be fast and furious. So, if you are taking beginners, ask the rink to suggest the best, least busy, time to go. As with the ice skating you can ask for private tuition.

Some roller rinks cater for birthday-party groups of all ages so, if that was your plan, ring up and ask for full details. If you do not want to skate, there are spectator facilities, and if some children come off the rink earlier than the others, there are usually video games provided.

The children will come off thirsty and probably quite hungry, so either come equipped with your own drinks and nibbles in the car, or be prepared to buy them refreshments.

Football Match

With all the recent problems at football matches you can't be blamed for not being very enthusiastic about this idea. A football outing needs careful organising. The best thing to do is to ring your local team (see Yellow Pages under Sports Clubs and Associations) and ask what they would recommend. Do not go when there is a local Derby on as these are the most likely trouble times. It is best to book seats for your group, and again be advised by the club as to where is the best place to sit. You will need to ring well in advance to find out when a suitable home match is being played. Don't try and take too many children in any case, and always go with sufficient number of helpers.

When you get into the vicinity of the stadium you will probably find that you have to park quite a distance away and walk to the entrance. It might be worth doing a recce before you park in order to discover where your particular entrance will be. You can then park as near as possible to that side of the stadium.

If the sun is not shining on your part you may find that sitting under cover in the shade

is quite cool, so ask the children to come with suitably warm clothing which they can always take off if they get too hot. If it is a chilly day we would recommend that you take a couple of travelling rugs, which could alternatively be used to soften the seating! It might be worthwhile taking a bag holding a few refreshments for during the match – if it were a freezing day you could take a flask of hot drink. When the match ends, depending on the number of spectators, it might be advisable to wait until the bulk of the crowd has disappeared before you start to move.

Always arrange with the children either a meeting point, or a contingency plan, if anybody gets separated from your group.

What you provide for tea following the match rather depends on how near the football stadium you live, and also on the weather. Perhaps you could plan to take a picnic (see pages 51–52) or wait until you get home, and have tea there (see pages 105–109). If it is a birthday treat have a football match cake (see page 108).

Horse Events

There are sure to be keen riders among your children, and friends who would relish a trip to a major three-day event, a point-to-point, or a horse show.

The best way to get information regarding dates of events is through horsey publications. Look out for point-to-point fixtures in the January edition. For summer events you will have to buy the March numbers. If you need a copy of a specialist magazine you'll have to book it in advance from a newsagent. Sometimes isolated newspaper orders never materialise, so if you want to be 100 per cent sure of getting a copy, write to the magazine's editorial office.

Take a picnic to any of these events and you'll have a good day out – weather permitting. If it is very cold, you will have to eat the picnic in the car – bring a thermos of hot soup, but don't be surprised if it is drunk by the adults and not the children.

There is always plenty to see even if you are not particularly horsey. Even the very young are catered for at our local point-to-point with a bouncey castle as the main attraction. Make up a party and go with another family or two. Always take waterproofs and, depending on the weather, rugs to sit on. If you don't arrive early you will have to be prepared to queue to get in, and also remember that it takes a while to leave these events too. Allow sufficient time in your schedule to cover possible delays.

Specific Shows

If your child has a favourite hobby or particular interest, you could use this as a basis for an outing party with a couple of similar minded friends: for example, to an air show (check with plane mags for dates and venues), science museum, safari park, tennis tournament. Or plan a day in London, Edinburgh or your nearest city, choosing two particular venues to visit – plus a trip to McDonald's, of course!

Leisure Centres

Most leisure centres are very good at organising children's parties, and it is certainly a wonderful way for energetic youngsters to let off steam. The usual arrangement is for the party organiser to get the children involved in activities such as trampolining, roller skating or football for perhaps half an hour. Then they get changed into swimming gear and swim for half an hour (but allow about 20 minutes for changing before and after). Then tea, which might be hamburgers and chips, Coca Cola and ice cream, usually provided by the leisure centre. Of course, you would be very welcome to provide your own cake if it is a birthday party.

Get in touch with your local leisure centre to see what they can organise and how much it will cost, then book your party well in advance. You may well find that there is more than one party taking place at the same time – but there is plenty of room in a leisure centre and this never seems to matter.

When you send out invitations to the party, enclose a short note explaining what the party will consist of and what the children should wear, for instance: 'Please come in a track suit, as we shall be roller skating and trampolining. Also please bring swimming things and towel (and arm bands if you can't swim) in a marked bag. NB: Please leave your watches at home.' Bring a list of your guests with you, so that you can check when everyone has arrived.

Be prepared to take an active part in the party – one party organiser won't be able to cope on his/her own. Wear track suits to help with the roller skating, etc, and change into swimming things with the children. It goes without saying that taking children swimming is a great responsibility, and you should be on the look-out for possible trouble the whole time. You may find that you can keep a closer eye on them from the edge of the pool, but if they are good swimmers you could enjoy a swim yourself and perhaps help organise a race or two.

Finally, if there are any gaps in the party (for instance while the children are waiting for their tea), it is better to organise a simple game or two, or perhaps running races, than to let them get over-excited by roaring round on their own.

The Cinema or Theatre

When you are planning a trip to a theatre or cinema, you will obviously want to choose the right level of entertainment for the age group you are catering for. Films are easier to choose than plays, as you will probably have heard about them anyway, or your children will have Also you have the age restrictions on the films to go by.

The choice of a play will also be dependent on the ages of the children involved. Don't expect teenagers to enjoy a marionette theatre, for example – some may, but most won't. Find out from the theatre if you are not sure what the plot, is, and discuss the childrens' ages with them. We were once disappointed taking some little girls to a ballet, which although it was entitled *Sleeping Beauty* turned out to be some rather way-out modern ballet, and not what any of us had bargained for. If there is any query, do a little research and then you won't be disappointed.

Some theatres are only too pleased for you to go backstage after a performance. You would have to enquire whether this was possible, but it is a great thrill if the staff are agreeable. When making your enquiry always state that it is for children and a birthday treat, or whatever. (Some theatres – the Royal Shakespeare Theatre, Stratford on Avon, for instance – organise backstage tours, but not necessarily after the performance.)

If you are thinking of taking a group of your child's friends to the cinema or theatre for a party treat, do remember before you ask half the class that it will be a costly exercise. Check with the box office whether they have any cheaper times – weekday matinees, perhaps – which you could take advantage of. If you are offered cheaper seats, check that there isn't a post in front of you all obscuring the view. Explain that you want seats that children will be able to see from – the staff are very helpful usually.

Consider what expenses you may incur when you get to the performance. You will want to buy a programme for each guest, and have something for them to nibble. Instead of buying expensive boxes of sweets, go armed with a polybag of goodies per child: a medley of little sweets, not sticky ones, which they can pick at during the performance. You will probably have to buy at least one drink per child in the interval. You could take individual fruit drinks or whatever, but children need to get up and stretch their legs, so they might as well go and buy a lolly or ice cream. Anyway, that is all part of the treat. (It might be a good idea to have a damp J-cloth for sticky fingers in a plastic bag in your handbag.)

When planning what meals to provide you will be governed by the time of the performance. If you are not taking many children, make it a special treat and turn it into a whole-day party. Keep the food simple, especially if you are having a supper at home after the performance. If you are going to an evening performance – and as the children get older, they would obviously prefer this – invite your guests to stay the night. It is so much easier than asking parents to turn out in the middle of the night, and also much more fun for the kids.

Camping Out

One of the greatest treats of all for younger children is to camp out for the night in your back garden. This could be organised with a few friends – if there is room in the garden for all their tents! Give them a barbecue supper and organise some games before they turn in for the night.

Be prepared for your night's sleep to be disturbed, though. This is partly because you may be sleeping lightly anyway – half keeping an ear out – and partly because, as sure as fate, someone will come in during the night. However, it is worth it as they do really enjoy themselves!

Tell your guests to bring tents, pillows, sleeping bags and torches, and have some spares available. Ideally, the tents should have attached ground sheets, but if there is one without you must put down some sort of waterproof base to prevent the sleeping bags going directly on to the ground. There probably won't be room in the tents for camp beds so you could offer eiderdowns, duvets or whatever you have available to go under the sleeping bags for added comfort – some may refuse

such luxury! We would also advise you to spray the children with insect repellent before they finally go to bed!

Make sure each tent has a torch. You will have to leave your back door open, and of course leave some lights on. Do make sure your garden is secure so that the children can't wander off. Tell them to leave their shoes or slippers by the tent entrance – then they won't find themselves lying on them and it will remind them to put them on when they go out.

Before you say goodnight stress that you won't mind at all if someone wants to give up half way through the night. (It's probably best if the tents are large enough to have two in a tent anyway.) Don't attempt this enterprise with children who are too young – probably not below the age of eight. And don't attempt it with boys and girls who are too old, either! With the eight-to-tens you should be all right. They must be really keen or they will be indoors in two seconds! If the children are still quite young perhaps Dad could be persuaded to sleep out there too . . .

Café Parties

Many chains of restaurants – The Happy Eater, McDonald's, Wimpy Bars, Little Chef, Pizzaland, as well as lots of local eating places – have now jumped on the party bandwaggon and will provide all you need in the way of food and decorations for your children's party. Sometimes they'll even lay on the cake and entertainment too. It does, of course, cost more than doing it at home, but if you have taken a fairly small group to, say, a swimming pool or football match, it can be a wonderful way to round off the day. Look up in the Yellow Pages (under Restaurants) for the address of your nearest eating place, and discuss the party with them. Not unreasonably, they usually like several days' notice.

Food for Outings and Picnics

Organisation is the key to a successful picnic outing. Make a careful checklist of all the food and bits and pieces you will need as you can't afford to leave anything behind. The following list is pretty comprehensive and would cover most eventualities, but some things you would obviously not require if you were just popping down the road. Whether you are taking a party on one of the outings discussed, to the local park or woods, or further afield, have sufficient helpers. This is especially relevant if you are walking there, crossing roads and clutching the picnic as well as a dozen little hands.

Food, itemised
Kitchen towel or paper napkins
Damp J-cloths in plastic bags
Plastic bag for rubbish
Basic first-aid kit, Waspeze and insect repellent spray
Sun-tan cream (depending on the weather!)
Rugs to sit on

Bottle opener (corkscrew if required!)
A spare set of children's clothes
Towel
Ball (especially if taking boys)
Whistle to round up the younger troops
Food, drink (and cutlery if required)
Washing-up bowl (could be useful in car journeys if someone feels ill, or just for giving the dog a drink!)
Bottle of plain water (for anyone feeling ill or dog to drink)
Telephone number of a parent to be contacted if you are delayed.

We found that the easiest way to cater is to pack a 'nose bag' or individual picnic for each child. You will find some food is wasted, but it takes all the hassle out of serving up the bits and bobs of a picnic. Collect up enough large plastic margarine or ice-cream boxes beforehand. Put a piece of kitchen roll at the bottom of each and pack with the food. Discuss with your children what they think would be the most popular food to include in this 'nose bag'.

Alternatively, if you are going with other families each could bring a separate part of the meal. Plan the whole thing together so that one person takes the main course, someone else puddings, someone else the drinks (if it is freezing weather, perhaps include some soup to warm everyone up). If you are leaving early, you will have to prepare your picnic the night before. This is fine, but just make sure that everything is cold, clingfilmed and refrigerated for the night.

Popular picnic food would include a selection from the following:

LUNCH

Chicken drumsticks. Frozen drumsticks can be bought in packs very reasonably. Cook them with butter and dried herbs for flavour, or roll in beaten egg and then breadcrumbs and fry for crunch! Try the devilled chicken drumstick recipe on page 110. Place a little clingfilm at the end of the bone – it will avoid those very greasy fingers.

Sausages. Chipolatas are easier for young children to eat than large sausages.

Pigs in a blanket (see page 110) are excellent served cold.

Scotch Egg or plain hard-boiled egg.

Slice of favourite bought pizza.

Soft roll, pre-buttered if required. See Match Party Food for some filling ideas.

Salad. Sticks of carrot, cucumber or celery, and quarters of tomato.

Packets of crisps, etc.

Piece of fruit.

Pudding. If you want to do a pudding have individual pots of fruit yoghurt, or make individual chocolate or lemon mousses (see page 83) in old yoghurt pots. Take plastic spoons. (It is probably best if you keep these out of the 'nose bag': if you have an insulated cold bag or box keep them in this, but don't forget to hand them out.) Simplest of all, buy everyone an ice cream.

TEA
2 sandwiches (make two sorts and give one of each)
2 chipolatas or one plus a mini sausage roll
1 packet each of crisps, Hula Hoops, etc.
Biscuits: try and avoid melting chocolate biscuits and give a KP chocolate dip to each with, say, a flapjack (see page 107).
Give each a separate cup cake perhaps piped with the child's name (see page 109).

Pieces of fruit
Mini packet of Smarties or raisins, etc.

See also Match Party Food.

DRINKS
Don't take too many fizzy drinks if travelling far. Try the following instead.

Flask of plain water

Individual cans or cartons of juices, plus straws. It may be more expensive to buy a selection of individual drinks but it is so much easier to hand them out, especially if somebody wants a drink while you are going along in the car.

Flasks of soft drinks. If you prefer to take the drink in flasks, use old yoghurt or cream pots for glasses.

Games for Journeys

Most of us would agree that long journeys, especially car journeys, are not much fun for younger children. Most of them dislike sitting still! Try all the sensible ideas like the odd stop, the occasional packet of sweets or biscuits (but not chocolate-covered ones) and cassette tapes of stories, pop music, etc. When you cannot take any more pop, or they get fed up with golden oldies, see if the following games can help to pass the time. They are all simple to learn and need no special props. The object is not so much the winning or losing, but rather keeping everyone amused. However, you can if you like award points in each game and keep a running total, ending the journey with a championship title. It depends on how competitive you are all feeling.

MAPS

This is not really a game, but does pass the time very constructively. Encourage the children to look at the map or road atlas – it makes the journey more interesting for them if they know where they are going, and where they are on the map. Get them to work out what the symbols on the map mean. Explain how the mileage scale works so that they can see how far they are going. Older children can help you to work out your route and navigate while you are driving.

ROAD SIGNS

Most road atlases have an illustrated page of road signs. Get the children to study these and then have a competition to see who can be the first to call out the meaning of the road signs as you drive past them. Younger children can each choose a particular sign (a 'T Junction' or a 'Stop sign') and see how many they can spot of their own sign.

HOMONYMS

Players have to think of words which are pronounced in the same way but spelt differently – place, plaice; whale, wail; current, currant, etc. Score one for single-syllable words, two for two syllables. This is a game that can last off and on for days.

MY AUNT ELLEN

One person thinks of something that Aunt Ellen hates (words containing the letter P, for instance), and says 'My Aunt Ellen loves cakes but hates pastry', 'My Aunt Ellen loves oranges, but hates apples', until the others guess the answer. They can ask questions if it helps them to guess.

AUNT JEMIMA

The first player starts off with 'Aunt Jemima went shopping and she bought a cabbage', the next player says 'Aunt Jemima went shopping and she bought a cabbage and a tin of shoe polish', and so on. Players who forget one of the items drop out until only one remains.

I SPY

A good game for younger children but don't choose objects such as gates or chimneys that flash past too quickly.

QUICK SPOTTING

Draw up a list of ten things you might see on a journey and award points for each one. For instance one point for a red car, two for a thatched cottage, three for a police car, ten for a Lamborghini, and so on, and the first person to see the object and shout out wins the points.

JUST A MINUTE

Play as in the radio game: a player has to talk on a topic – chosen by the driver who is chairman – for one minute without repetition, hesitation or deviation.

CAR NUMBER PLATES

Use the letters in the number plate of the car in front to make a phrase or sentence, including the names of the people in your car if possible – ELB, 'Edward loves blancmange'. This is another game that can be played on and off for days.

CAR NUMBERS

Call out the number of the car in front and the first person to add them up correctly scores a point: for instance 682 = 16, and so on (or for younger brothers or sisters get them to spot their own age in a number, 4 in 241, for instance. This is especially good in a town with lots of traffic about).

HANGMAN

The object in this word-making game is to avoid being the last person who is obliged to finish the word. The first player says a letter, say, 'L', the next person says 'E', the next 'M' and so on, until the word is formed, in this case LEMON. Any player can challenge, when it is his turn, if he thinks the previous player is merely guessing and not spelling a real word. You are also out if you accidentally produce a shorter complete word within the longer word 'Yes' in 'Yesterday', for instance.

CAPITAL CITIES

The first player thinks of a capital city beginning with 'A', Addis Abbada, the next thinks of one beginning with 'B', Brussels, and so on. An easier version is to play by using the name of any town, not just capital cities. You can also play the game with boys' names, Angus, Bernard, etc, or girls' names, Amy, Bernadette, or invent your own ideas for lists.

BOOM

Everyone can play this. Players take it in turns to count, but the number 6, or numbers where it appears, say 16, are replaced by the word 'boom'. Count as fast as you can and as soon as you make a mistake the next player takes over. A more difficult version is to omit multiples of the number, this would mean leaving out 12, 18, 24, and so on – good practice for learning tables!

LINKED NAMES

Choose one kind of name – boys' names, towns, countries and so on – and then everyone in turn has to think of a name in which the first letter is the last of the one before, for instance, France, Egypt, Tunisia, Austria, and so on. Anyone who can't think of a name is out.

MESSAGES

Think of a word – not too long – and everyone has to make a sentence using the letters of the word (in the same order). For instance the word 'flower' might make:

'Fred loves outings with elephant rides'

or 'Fetch Lucy our wooden-eared rabbit'

It's always hard to decide on a winner as everyone likes their own effort the best!

SONGS

These songs all go on for a long time and can be sung over and over again, and so help shorten the journey. They are all old favourites, easy to learn and great fun to sing. Try taking a verse each in turn, and award points for the one who sings it best – or worst.

One man went to mow

One man went to mow
Went to mow a meadow
One man and his dog
Went to mow a meadow

Two men went to mow
Went to mow a meadow
Two men, one man and his dog
Went to mow a meadow
Etc, etc.

Ten green bottles

Ten green bottles standing on the wall
Ten green bottles standing on the wall
If one green bottle should accidentally fall
There'd be nine green bottles standing on
  the wall

Nine green bottles standing on the wall
Nine green bottles standing on the wall
If one green bottle should accidentally fall . . .
  Etc, etc.

Green grow the rushes-o

I'll sing you one-o!
Green grow the rushes-o!
What is your one-o?
One is one and all alone and ever more
  shall be so.

I'll sing your two-o!
Green grow the rushes-o!
What is your two-o?
Two, two, the lily-white boys, clothed all in
  green-o
One is one and all alone and ever more
  shall be so.

I'll sing you three-o!
Green grow the rushes-o!
What is your three-o?
Three, three the rivals,
Two, two, the lily-white boys, clothed all in
  green-o
One is one and all alone and ever more
  shall be so.

The following verses are:

Four for the gospel makers
Five for the symbols at your door
Six for the six proud walkers
Seven for the seven stars in the sky
Eight for the April rainers
Nine for the nine bright shiners
Ten for the Ten Commandments
Eleven for the eleven who went to heaven
Twelve for the twelve apostles.

There's a hole in my bucket

1. There's a hole in my bucket, dear Liza,
     dear Liza,
   There's a hole in my bucket, dear Liza,
     a hole.
2. Then mend it dear Henry, dear Henry,
     dear Henry,
   Then mend it, dear Henry, dear Henry,
     mend it!
3. With what shall I mend it, dear Liza . . .
     with what?
4. With a straw, dear Henry . . . a straw.
5. The straw is too long, dear Liza . . . too long.
6. Then cut it, dear Henry . . . cut it.
7. With what shall I cut it, dear Liza . . .
     with what?
8. With a knife, dear Henry . . . a knife.
9. The knife is too blunt, dear Liza . . . too
     blunt.
10. Then sharpen it, dear Henry . . .
     sharpen it.
11. With what shall I sharpen it, dear
     Liza . . . with what?
12. With a stone, dear Henry . . . a stone.
13. The stone is too dry, dear Liza . . . too dry.
14. Then wet it, dear Henry . . . wet it.
15. With what shall I wet it, dear Liza . . .
     with what?
16. With water, dear Henry . . . with water.
17. In what shall I get it, dear Liza . . . in what?
18. In a bucket, dear Henry . . . in a
     bucket
19. (All together) 'There's a hole in my
     bucket, dear Liza . . . A HOLE!!'

She'll be coming round the mountain

She'll be coming round the mountain when
  she comes
She'll be coming round the mountain when
  she comes
She'll be coming round the mountain
Coming round the mountain
Coming round the mountain when she
  comes

She'll be wearing pink pyjamas when she
  comes . . .

She'll be riding six white horses when she
  comes . . .

Make up your own additional verses.

Family Parties

Midsummer, Hallowe'en, Guy Fawkes or Hogmanay parties could be the excuse for small or large family gatherings, but you don't need any particular reason for an informal meal followed by some fun games. There are many occasions when it's a nice idea to invite a couple of other families (or more, if you have space) for a lunch or supper: for example, the boat race, FA Cup Final or the Grand National.

Don't worry too much about the children's ages coinciding exactly – obviously there must be some who are comparable with your children but you will be surprised how the teenagers will have a giggle with the six-year-olds in this sort of atmosphere. These parties are a good way for you to entertain easily and casually, and for the children to experience and learn to socialise – great for family togetherness. You can get everybody involved in the preparations, but keep things simple as it is not a grand lunch or dinner party you are planning, but a family get-together! If you are likely to be pushed for time, the children can make a fruit salad or simple mousse for pudding. And if you cannot face the messy kitchen following that exercise, ask the other families who are coming to bring something. Share the work load, and everyone can have fun.

The menu we provide is for a gathering of about fourteen people for a casual supper or lunch. However, we have included lots of other ideas for larger parties, with page references for the recipes at the end of the book.

The children will want you to join in with them, so don't go and nod off in the sitting room or chatter exclusively amongst yourselves. You must prepare to have family entertainment. The children can help organise. Here are a few ideas for you to work on.

Sporting Events

If the party is planned round a sporting occasion, run some sort of a sweepstake. For example, if you were having a Grand National party cut the names of all the runners out of a newspaper and put them in a hat. Everyone then has an interest in the race, and those who pick out the winner, second, third or fourth could either be given a little present, or perhaps some money. If there are more runners than guests, then give them two chances. For the Boat Race, ask your guests to take either a dark or pale blue ribbon from a hat – allow equal numbers of ribbon for Oxford and for Cambridge. The two teams which result will have some definite allegiance and whichever team loses could pay a forfeit – acting a charade for the others, or doing the washing up! Later, use the team divisions for playing games (see page 64).

In summertime have a family tennis match

– depending on ages, have fathers and daughters against mothers and sons. The others can ball-boy and umpire, and the finals can be between the winner of each group. Finish up with a barbecue at home (see page 67). Look up the tennis-match section to devise a proper tournament if your numbers are large.

New Year's Eve Party

New Year's Eve can be a problem when you have children who are old enough to enjoy staying up, but perhaps not old enough to be left without a babysitter (a rare commodity on New Year's Eve). Solve the problem by inviting in some friends with children of a similar age to your own, and both generations can enjoy bringing in the New Year.

Sort out some Scottish reels. You must have a caller who really knows what they are doing. If necessary ask for information from the dancing teacher at school. You'll need the right records or tapes, of course. Run a disco as well for a break from the reels. Try the cold chicken concoction (see page 114) for a buffet supper, or a lasagne (see page 100) if you have room to sit everybody down.

Hallowe'en Party

If your guests are the right sort of age, they will enjoy wearing fancy dress. Try out the following ideas:

GHOST
Use a small sheet to cover the 'ghost' completely. Cut eye holes and fasten a piece of elastic around the back of the head to hold the sheet in place. If you have any old black net, cover the sheet with this to give a very ghostly effect.

WITCH AND WIZARD
You need long black, purple or red cloaks (old curtains?), tall witches' hats (make these out of black card, and cover with stick-on stars and moons). Colour faces white, and add black lines and red lips with face paints, and black out teeth with mascara. Witches could paint their fingernails with black nail varnish. If you have a small besom broom let the witch carry this.

VAMPIRE
A long cloak (as above), white shirt and black trousers is all you will need. Get a set of plastic fangs from a toyshop and have lips and chin dripping with blood (face paint!)

SKELETONS
Paint white bones on to an old black jersey and tights.

Older children dislike wearing fancy dress, so don't try to persuade them. However, they may be willing to wear long cloaks, which will add to the spooky atmosphere and keep them warm if you are out of doors.

Get your decorations ready in good time. Use pumpkins if you can find them – hollow them out, make holes for eyes and mouth and put nightlights inside. Don't worry if you can't get hold of pumpkins – turnips will do, or even sugar beet, if you live in the country. When you have hollowed them out, turn them upside down so that they have a flat base to stand on. Another idea is to put night lights inside ordinary jam jars: you can stick coloured tissue paper around the outside for extra effect. All these lights can be used in the house or the garden, but make sure they are well out of harm's way. You may well be lucky with your weather and decide to start the party off out of doors with a bonfire. Put a baking tray filled with chestnuts into the embers (prick with a fork first) – but only adults should fish them out, and with long tongs.

In the house, change some of your light bulbs to red, orange or blue, or cover the old ones with paint. This gives a very ghostly light.

Go round the local dress shops well before the party and persuade them to lend you some of the old mannequins used in the shop windows. Dress them up as witches and skeletons, etc, and have them hanging on the walls or sitting in a chair.

Include among your games such traditional ones such as apple-bobbing and doughnut-chomping.

BLINDFOLD FEELING GAME

Each player is blindfolded in turn and led into a separate room to identify a collection of objects by touch: a peeled grape (tell them it is a witch's eye), cold spaghetti (Medusa's hair), avocado pear skin (frog's skin), avocado stone (a Cyclop's eye). We won't give you any more ideas here or the adults will know them all – the children are very clever at thinking up their own. You can extend this game by making it a smelling and tasting game as well: fill saucers with coffee, curry powder, tomato ketchup, chocolate sauce, etc. When each player has had his go, they can sit and watch the others, but they must not shout out the answers!

Make the room for this game very ghostly with dim lights and weird noises, but if any of the younger children are at all frightened, let them help you blindfold the others rather than making them play themselves. Your children will enjoy recording a tape of weird noises in advance to play back during the party.

APPLE-BOBBING

Play this in the kitchen! Put a large bowl or bucket of water on the floor and float apples in it. Players have to pick up the apples with their teeth (hands behind the back). The winner is the one who gets most apples in a particular time limit.

DOUGHNUT-CHOMPING

Thread doughnuts on pieces of string, and fasten string to a broom handle or pole. Attach the pole to the ceiling or across two doors, if you can. If not, balance it between two chair backs. Players have to eat the doughnuts with their hands behind their backs. First to finish is the winner.

Also see page 61 for lots more games.
Serve a buffet supper. Dips and crisps, Devilled Chicken Drumsticks and a profiterole pyramid, for instance. If you want to serve a hot drink, serve the Mulled Mystery on page 119 – it is quite delicious. Otherwise serve a fizzy apple or orange punch, but have a look through the drinks section first. Give all the guests a toffee apple to take home.

Firework Party

You can choose one of two sorts of firework party. Bearing in mind that fireworks are both dangerous and expensive, the first option is to arrange to meet some other families at a local firework display and then come back home for supper. Have some indoor fireworks and sparklers to finish the evening off for the children. The second option is to have a party at home which is so well organised that the risk of accidents is minimal. Make it a 'bring a firework' party to cut down the cost a bit.

If a display is to be worthwhile you will find the cost horrendous, so ask those who are coming to provide a couple of fireworks per person and you will at least have a basis for the display. One or two big fireworks are better than a box of small ones. Ask guests to deliver their contributions a couple of days ahead of the party to allow you time to organise the order of fireworks and devise a good varied display. Order your own fireworks well ahead of the date of the party. Always organise your props – posts for catherine wheels, etc – in the daylight, even the weekend before the party. Don't try to rush home a bit early on the day to organise things. The display will be a disappointment, and the person in charge will be in a flap (this could be dangerous). Make sure that there is one person, with a helper, who is specifically in charge of the fireworks.

Write yourself a plan, and list the fireworks and where they are to be positioned. Don't forget equipment such as torches, matches and a bucket of water or sand. Make sure the guests and children are standing well away from the actual display area and, if possible, have the area roped off. Ask a friend to look after your pets indoors.

Get the children to make the Guy (not out of their father's best suit!), and build the bonfire where the spectators can be warmed by it. Don't light the bonfire before the guests arrive – it's amazing how quickly it will burn out. If you are inviting a lot of people, serve your food and mulled drinks while the display is going on – then with any luck you need not have them indoors at all (thus avoiding millions of gumboots marks over the kitchen floor). The children can help hand everything round. Why not make bowls of popcorn and hand them round too?

When the display has finished give the younger children a couple of sparklers each. This is a good way of ending the evening. Alternatively, once the fireworks are over, have everyone indoors to eat supper. This way they stay longer and perhaps you can play some family games (see page 62). The food you serve will depend on the type of party you plan, and the time at which it is held. Adapt these general suggestions to suit your particular party. The recipes are at the back of the book.

If food is outside:
Hotdogs
Chicken Drumsticks
Beefburgers in rolls
Baked Potatoes cut into manageable pieces
Pizza Fingers
followed by chocolate biscuits.

If food is inside:
Stew
Lasagne
Shepherds' Pie
Baked Potatoes
followed by Chocolate Mousse.

Provide jugs of mulled drinks (for children's recipe see page 119) and have a jug of orange squash in case of need.

Barn Dance

You must have a suitable venue for this party, but even more important is to book an experienced and enthusiastic caller and an equally good band. A party like this could be a disaster if you don't have somebody competent in charge. We heard of an occasion where the caller kept looking at his notes, trying to keep everybody going but failing dismally. Nobody enjoyed themselves.

Ideally you should contact a caller and band through personal recommendation but the Yellow Pages (under Dance Bands) might list a suitable group. Failing all else you could ask a local dancing teacher, or go through an agency – see Yellow Pages under Entertainment Agencies (you will incur an agency fee, though). Wherever you find your band, double check how successful they are, and ask for references and take them up. Make certain, too, that the band can cope with mixed age groups.

Remember to ask your band how long a break they will be taking during the evening so that you can plan the party. You might like to serve supper during the break, or have food available all evening. If you have a running buffet, play some disco music while the band has a break. Perhaps you could rig up a hi-fi system with some tapes, depending on the venue.

DECORATIONS
If you are lucky enough to have access to a real barn for this party, put straw bales around for everyone to sit on (so long as you are particularly strict about no smoking). Otherwise decorate your room, garage or hall with streamers, balloons in a net, etc. If you could get hold of any Western posters these would be fun, but remember that anything too small will not make much impact in a large hall.

FOOD AND DRINK
Serve simple food that can all be eaten with the fingers. The children could label the food with appropriate names, for example, 'Bunk House Burgers' (beef burger in a roll, see page 110), 'Sheriff's Sausages' (sausages on sticks, see page 74) 'Cowboy's Chicken' (chicken drumsticks, see page 110). For very large numbers, see discothèque food, page 110.

Everyone will get very thirsty, so have plenty of drink available. A fruit cup is always popular.

Family Party Food

Throughout the book we have stressed that you should keep everything very simple, whatever kind of party you are holding. If you are having a casual get-together at home perhaps the easiest thing would be to serve finger foods for the children to hand round instead of a starter. Then have the main food in the kitchen as a buffet; take your plates and sit down at one table together if possible. This way you will get more of a party atmosphere. Younger childen will love making place names and organising the seating plan.

MENU
Mini Sausage Rolls
Cheese Straws
Dips

★★★★★★★★★★

Meat Fondue
Cold Chicken Concoction
Beef Casserole

★★★★★★★★★

Salad
Baked Potatoes

★★★★★★★★★

Chocolate Mousse (see page 83)
Pavlova (see page 81)
Ice Cream with Various Sauces
(see page 104)

Indoor Games

The games suggested here incorporate some for young children, some for older children and some for all the family to play. You will have to choose what is best for your occasion.

Always plan your games in advance rather than trying to organise them at the time. You will probably find that you will not get through them quite as fast as you did when the children were younger. However, have plenty planned! Have prizes ready for the younger groups. Make a list of the games you intend to play as your mind can go blank so easily – it's not only the children who are getting older, we all are! By each game jot down what props you will need, then you can get the children to organise them for you!

BABYFACE
For this game you will need a piece of board made of wood or hardboard, or a pin board and Blu Tack. Provide your guests with a piece of paper and a pencil each. Ask everyone to bring a photograph of themselves as a baby. One of your family must be in charge of collecting the photographs when everybody arrives, and Blu-Tacking them on to the board with a number underneath each photograph. Everyone then has to guess who is who. Whoever is in charge of the game then marks the papers, and whoever has scored most wins. Remind everybody to name their papers, otherwise you won't know whose is whose.

MUSICAL CHAIRS (WITH A DIFFERENCE)
Instead of just having chairs, use the odd chair, cushions, bean bags, rug, pillow, anything you have to hand. (If you are having a coloured theme to your party, try to find things in

Our recipes are for fourteen, so adapt the quantities to suit your requirements. They are designed for everyone to eat, so they are not too sophisticated in case there are much younger children involved. Whatever food you serve, try to ensure that you have a selection which can appeal to adults and children alike: for example, serve cold chicken which you can dress up with a sauce, or serve plain and simple for the less adventurous. If the weather is fine, the ideal way to entertain one and all in an unsophisticated way is to hold a barbecue.

Try a fondue party. The advantage of this particular meal is that it helps breaks the ice and gets everybody chattering together. Add another dimension by playing forfeits if anyone drops their meat into the cooking oil, for example, kiss the person on their left.

matching colours.) Put all these objects in the middle of the room and the participants have to dance to disco music around them, and when the music stops grab whatever form of seating they can, and sit on it. You remove one item of seating after each go, and whoever is in last wins.

PICTURE GALLERY

Put photos of famous faces on a board, or Blu-Tack them to a wall having written a number in the corner of each photograph. Give the children a pencil and paper each and whoever guesses the most faces, wins.

JIGSAW PUZZLE GAME

Cut up advertisements from magazines into two or three pieces, depending on the participants' ages, etc. Keep one piece back to give to each person and hide the others around the house. Whoever collects most advertisements wins. Alternatively use old Christmas or birthday cards for the jigsaws.

STATUES, MUSICAL

It is quite fun to play musical statues the wrong way round. Stand still when the music is playing and dance when it stops! If anyone moves when the music is playing they are out, and whoever is in last wins.

PASS THE PARCEL IN REVERSE

Wrap up one small present, and put a heap of paper bags or carrier bags, or whatever sort of mixed bags you want, in the middle of a circle of children. Give one child the wrapped present to pass round. Each time the music stops the child with the present has to put another bag on to it. The person who puts the last bag on gets the prize, which they then have to unwrap! NB. Use smallest bags first.

PASS THE PARCEL WITH FORFEITS

You will need to wrap up a conventional pass-the-parcel parcel with enough layers for each guest to unwrap one and, if you wish, you can tape a sweet to each layer. However, instead of just passing the parcel and grabbing the sweet, they will have to perform a forfeit as well. Make up your list of forfeits prior to the party: for example, imitate Maggie Thatcher at Question Time, say the seven-times table backwards, and so on.

RAILWAY CARRIAGES

You will need to provide a newspaper per guest and, in advance of your party, muddle up the pages of the newspaper. It is only fair to have identical newspapers for the children, as some are so much larger and more difficult to cope with than others. The first player to get the newspaper back into correct page order wins the game.

CHOPPING CHOCOLATE GAME

You will need a plate, a knife and fork, a pair of gloves, a hat, a scarf, a dice and a large bar of chocolate unwrapped. The children have to throw the dice and when a player throws a six, he/she puts on the hat, the scarf and the gloves, and tries to chop the chocolate (which can be eaten if successfully chopped)! In the meantime, the other children are throwing the dice, and if anybody else scores a six the person chopping has to give up all the equipment and the next one has a go. (There is no real winner to this game.)

TREASURE HUNT

You can play this individually or in pairs. Give each a list of items to find. Also give them a pencil with which to write where each item is (keep a 'master' list to yourself). Let the whole house be used as it's so much more fun. Have at least twelve items. Whoever finds them all first is the winner. Examples of what to hide might include:

Piece of Elastoplast	A nut
Piece of sticky tape	An elastic band
A Polo mint	A button
A safety pin	An egg

HAPPY HELMES HOUSE GAME

You can play this game as individuals or in pairs. Give clues, preferably in rhyming couplets, to objects to be found around the house. Each person (or pair) has a photocopy of the clues on which he (or they) writes the answers. The winner is the first person to discover the word which is made up from the first letters of the answers to the clues. To make the game more difficult, muddle the order of the clues so that it becomes an anagram. Adapt your clues to suit the age group of your guests.

As an example, here is a list of nine clues, with answers which make up the word 'Wednesday'.

1. Look behind the yellow curtain
   Of the answer, you'll be certain. — **W**indow

2. In a cupboard on the wall
   You'll find some help if you should fall. — **E**lastoplast

3. *You must not look* – remember well.
   When you came in was there a bell?
   A knocker on the door? A chime?
   A trumpet? Banger? Squeaky toys?
   What have we put to make a noise? — **D**oorknocker, door bell, etc.

4. Tis now the last day of the year,
   What sort of party have we here? — **N**ew Eve's Year

5. Look in the desk and you will discover
   Along with the paper a useful cover. — **E**nvelope

6. They have their ups and downs you know,
   Eleven standing in a row,
   Another four, lead to the floor,
   They help you to your bedroom go. — **S**tairs

7. In a room where we feel dozy
   These cover us up and keep us cosy. — **D**uvet

8. There was a young lady of Ryde,
   Who ate a green . . . ? and died.
   The . . . ? fermented,
   Inside the lamented,
   And made cider in side her inside.
   (There's a bowl of these in the dining room) — **A**pple

9. In a cool place you must seek,
   These pots will keep at least a week. — **Y**oghurt

TASTING GAME

You will need a blindfold and about ten morsels to taste – jam, toothpaste, carrot, chocolate, etc – a spoon and pencil and paper for each guest. You give each guest a taste of each and they have to go out and write down what they think they have eaten. The winner is the one who gets most correct.

WHAT'S IN ROSIE'S BOX?

You will need one large box, prepared with a hole on top and half of a pair of tights stapled to the hole so that no one can see inside. Inside the box will be eight items – a coin, a piece of string, a piece of ice (put this in just before you play the game), etc. Give each guest a pencil and paper. Each player puts a hand in the leg of the tights in the box and identifies what they can feel inside. They have two minutes (you will be timekeeper) to feel, and then they must write down what they remember. Whoever gets most right is the winner.

TRAY GAME

You will need a tray with twelve items on it – a pen, a paperclip, a rubber, a book, etc. If you are giving a party with a colour theme, again continue this by making sure that all the items are, for example, pink. Give each child a pencil and a piece of paper. Show them the tray with the items on for a certain time, then take the tray away and allow them two minutes in which they have to remember and write down all the items you showed them. Whoever remembers most, wins. Be prepared for a tied win and have several little prizes ready.

FATHERS' KNEES

This is not a team game, it is just good fun. The fathers go into a separate room, the doorway of which can easily be seen by the remaining families. A rug is pinned over the top two-thirds of the doorway.

The fathers take off their trousers and tie beribboned rosettes below their knees. They then, one at a time, parade their legs, incognito, past the doorway. The families guess which pair of legs belongs to each father.

Indoor Team Games

There are many ways of dividing everyone into teams and it is a good idea to organise this when guests first arrive. Pop a 'team' sticker (the children will love organising this) on everybody. They can be bought at any good stationer's, or use coloured labels for a cheaper version. Alternatively make badges, and use different colours or shapes for your teams. Other ideas for team divisions could be animals (pigs, cows, sheep, mice) or TV soap operas (*Dallas, Dynasty, Coronation Street, East Enders*), and so on. If you are having a family party, you could pre-match the teams and make yourself a list: put a parent with his own shy child; a father in each team; split similar aged children. Alternatively have the children versus the adults, in which case give the adults some sort of handicap.

PASS THE ORANGE

You will need two oranges. Give each captain an orange. He or she puts it under their chin, and passes it down the line. A variation of this is for the two teams to lie on the floor, and to pass the orange between their ankles.

PASS THE MATCHBOX

You will need two matchbox covers. Give the captain of each team a matchbox, and then the guests have to pass the matchbox on their noses along the line, without using their hands. Whichever team finishes first is the winner.

PASS THE BALLOON

You will need two balloons, and two spares or more! Give each team leader a balloon. The team leader puts the balloon between his knees and passes it to the next person in the line, and so on. Neither team has won until the last member has burst the balloon. Alternatively pass small balloons under chins.

CHARADES

Give each team a list of suitable subjects – book or film titles, etc – and a few minutes to think about them. Then each team acts them to the other team within a set time-limit. A variation on this game is to let each team suggest a word, for example a three-syllable word, such as candlelit. They then act out each syllable. The team then acts a little play, the first act of which includes in the dialogue the first syllable, and so on. Then the final act must include the whole word.

TEAM TICKLES

You will need lots of string and two dessertspoons for two teams. Have two very long pieces of string (the length depending on the number of your guests). With the dessertspoon tied to the end of each piece, the first team member has to 'thread' the spoon under their clothes, downwards, and pass the spoon to the next member who threads it similarly upwards! The first person has to hold on to the end of the piece of string so that it doesn't get pulled through and out. The first team to sit down, all joined together, is the winner.

TEAM 'TRIVIAL PURSUITS'

If you have the general knowledge game 'Trivial Pursuits', play this as a team game. Each side has a box of questions. Choose two team leaders. The captains keep score cards, so

provide two pencils and pieces of paper. All the questions on each card are asked by one team of the other. A member from one team asks the first set of questions of the other team. The team captain gives the final answer to the questions, after a general discussion amongst all the members of the opposing team. Everybody has an opportunity to put the list of questions. After a round (when the questions from one card have all been answered), the opposing team then has the chance to put the questions on their first card to the other team.

GENERAL KNOWLEDGE QUIZ

It is probably kinder to make this a team game in case anyone gets a fit of nerves and can't answer a single question. Have a list of general knowledge questions and pencil and paper for each team.

BARK IN THE DARK

This game is played in the dark with two teams. Before the party, write out two identical lists of animals or birds and the noises they make for instance, horse = neigh, pig = grunt, owl = twit twoo, and so on. Give each team leader a list, making sure that there are enough noises to go round. The leader then whispers the name and noise of an animal to each individual team member.

Take the teams to separate parts of the house, and turn out all the lights. In the darkness each person shouts out their appropriate noise (moo, hiss, meow, twit-twoo, etc) and finds his 'partnered noise'. When the partner is found, hang on to them and stop making the noise. The last two to pair up are then the only ones making a noise and have lost. The lights are turned on and they do a forfeit such as blind man's feast, when two people (both blindfolded) feed each other jelly whilst sitting cross-legged on a table.

DRAWING GAME

Divide your guests into teams. The host lists simple objects or ideas such as cold, happy, light, etc. If there were four teams he would need four lists of, say, twenty objects. He retains the list. Each team sends off to the host one member, who is given the name of an object on his team's list. He returns to his group and without speaking or miming, he draws the object as best he can. As soon as another member of his team has guessed it, even if it is only partly drawn, the next team member runs off to the host to collect the next object. He will first have to confirm that the previous answer was correct, before being given his turn. The first team to guess all the objects on its list wins. Adapt our lists as you wish.

North	South	East	West
Owl	Peacock	Swallow	Parrot
Mouse	Beetle	Bee	Ladybird
Camel	Cow	Giraffe	Elephant
Sun	Saturn	Moon	Star
Sheep	Pig	Cat	Rabbit
Leek	Cabbage	Marrow	Pea pod
Car	Train	Army tank	Ship
Snow	Rain	Fog	Cloud
Spoon	Fork	Knife	Cup
Volcano	Wave	Whirlwind	Bomb
Tin can	Dustbin	Bottle	Sack
See-saw	Swing	Slide	Circus
Parson	Queen	King	Bride
Sickle	Hammer	Nail	Scissors
Violin	Piano	Trumpet	Saxophone

DICTIONARY GAME

One team looks up a very unusual word in the dictionary. Each member of the team then gives a definition of this word. One of the meanings is the correct one. The other team has to decide whose answer is correct. The points are scored when a team guesses the right answer.

LOO ROLL GAME

Choose two captains, and divide the guests into two teams. Give each team a roll of loo paper and whoever can wrap up their captain first in the loo roll is the winner. This is very popular!

TISSUE RACE

This is a team race and you will need two tissues (have some spares in case of need) and give each member of both teams a drinking straw. Have a start and finish line. The object of the race is to blow the tissue along the ground with the straw. Once over the finishing line the next member of the team gets going, and whichever team finishes first is the winner.

SARDINES

This is a good game to finish off with, involving everyone. It must be played in the dark, and it is probably wise, therefore, to restrict the area in your home where the participants can go without doing damage. One person goes and hides, then after a certain length of time everybody else sets out to find him or her, and hides there too. Complete silence should be maintained, although this becomes rather difficult when everyone is squashed up together!

Preparing food for the barbecue (see page 68).

'Pass the Balloon' teams in action.

An occasion for a family party (see page 59).

A giant inflatable or a bouncy castle will always get them going.

Barbecues

Barbecues are becoming increasingly popular, in spite of our uncertain weather. The reasons for this are not difficult to find: food tastes wonderful when cooked and eaten out of doors, and the cooking itself is such fun that everyone wants to lend a hand, especially the men, which is a wonderful break for habitual female cooks. In fact, some mothers have a barbecue practically every weekend in the summer because they find it such a wonderful way to get out of doing the cooking! Older (sensible) children can certainly help with the cooking, but it goes without saying that there must be an adult around at all times to supervise the barbecue itself. A fire which is hot enough to cook food is certainly hot enough to burn over-eager fingers.

The first thing you need is a suitable place for the barbecue. Out of doors, of course, not too far from the house because of all the fetching and carrying, and preferably in a sheltered place so that the wind won't blow the smoke into the house or straight to where you are planning to eat. Have a table alongside for all your cooking utensils, meat, seasoning, etc.

You can buy very attractive fully equipped barbecues of varying sizes, which have the added advantage of being mobile, but they are rather expensive. There is in fact nothing easier than building your own barbecue, either a temporary or a permanent one, for very little cost.

Charcoal is the conventional fuel for a barbecue. Buy it in the form of small briquettes, or as charcoal pieces. You can buy bags from most hardware shops, and it is certainly convenient to use and to store. But you don't need to use charcoal. Indeed, most kinds of wood, dried and cut small, will make a good barbecue – and can be easier to light and hotter than charcoal. Some people prefer the flavour of food cooked over a wood fire.

To light the barbecue, take off the top metal grid, crumple up some newspaper on the lower shelf, arrange kindling wood or a firelighter on top (or both, if you are a pessimist) and then a good layer of fuel, either charcoal or wood, on top. If you prefer you can buy special barbecue firelighters. When you have lit the fire, keep an eye on it until you see that the fuel itself has caught and is burning well. On no account encourage it with paraffin or petrol. Quite apart from the danger, it will make the food taste horrible.

Make sure you light your barbecue a good hour before you need to start the cooking. The flames should all have died down, leaving a pile of glowing embers, but don't forget to add fuel from time to time to keep the heat up. Replace the top metal grid to give it time to heat through. Allow enough time after the ember stage in which to cook the food. There is nothing worse than having hungry guests standing around while you prod chicken legs that you know quite well are still horribly raw in the middle! Get your cooking utensils together before the start, as well. You will need a jug of water (to sprinkle a few drops on the occasional flame), a small bowl of cooking oil and a pastry brush with which to baste the meat as it cooks, a pair of cooking tongs and, if possible, some sprigs of rosemary, sage, thyme, a bay leaf or two, or other herbs to give a lovely flavour to the food as it cooks.

Food

As with all parties, planning in advance for a barbecue is the secret of success. You don't want to be stuck in the kitchen while the family or guests are out of doors (hopefully) enjoying the sunshine.

If you are marinating the meat, then do this the night before and leave it in the fridge, turning it occasionally. Then make the barbecue sauce and leave it in the saucepan to reheat quickly. Then prepare the garlic bread, baked potatoes, etc, and finally the salad (but don't add any dressing until you are ready to serve). If you are entertaining a large number of guests, why not start cooking the meat and potatoes indoors and finish off on the barbecue, so you won't have so long to wait for them all to cook, especially if your barbecue is a small one?

We give the recipes in some detail for the benefit of younger cooks. You can, if you like, plan the whole meal from this section – the meat, the vegetables and the pudding – or you can serve a salad with the main course and ice cream for pudding – try one of the sauces on page 104 to go with it. These barbecue recipes are for eight people.

MARINADES FOR MEAT

If you are cutting the meat up (for kebabs, say) then do this first. Marinate the meat for several hours, or even overnight, turning occasionally. Use what is left of the marinade for basting the meat while cooking.

HERB MARINADE

3 tablespoons salad oil
1 tablespoon vinegar
1 clove garlic, crushed
2 teaspoons chopped mixed herbs, fresh or dried (thyme, rosemary, oregano, marjoram, etc.)
a pinch of salt and pepper

Mix all the ingredients. Put the meat into a shallow dish and pour the marinade over. Turn several times.

SPICY MARINADE

3 tablespoons salad oil
1 tablespoon soy sauce
2 cloves garlic, crushed
1 tablespoon brown sugar
1 teaspoon ground ginger
$\frac{1}{2}$ teaspoon dry mustard

A delicious zingy marinade, especially good with spare ribs. Mix all the ingredients, as above.

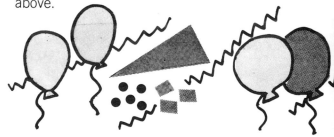

BARBECUE SAUCES

These should be made in advance to allow the flavour to develop. Reheat in a saucepan (on the cooker indoors, because it's so much easier) and pour a little over the meat just before serving. Serve the rest in a jug so that people can help themselves. You can also use these to baste the meat while it is cooking. Make a large quantity of the sauces if you like, to use when needed, as they will keep very well in a sealed jar in the fridge.

VERY EASY BARBECUE SAUCE

1 small tin concentrated tomato soup
2 tablespoons tomato ketchup
2 tablespoons vinegar
2 tablespoons pickle
1 tablespoon brown sugar
2 teaspoons Worcestershire sauce

Mix all the ingredients in a pan and simmer gently for a few minutes.

HERB-FLAVOURED BARBECUE SAUCE

5 tablespoons tomato ketchup
1 onion, chopped very fine
1 clove garlic, crushed
1 tablespoon fresh mixed herbs
1 tablespoon vinegar
1 tablespoon brown sugar
1 teaspoon Worcestershire sauce
a pinch of salt and pepper
$\frac{1}{2}$ bay leaf

Combine all the ingredients in a pan. Simmer slowly until onion is soft. Remove bay leaf before serving.

HOT FLAVOURED BREADS

Children love these breads, but don't serve them before the meat is ready, otherwise they will all be gone before the meal has started. Take a long French loaf, and cut it downwards every 2 inches (5 cm) along the loaf, but not right through, then spread one of the following flavoured butters between the slices. Wrap up firmly in foil and heat at the bottom of the oven for half an hour. You can buy herb, garlic or anchovy purée in tubes from most good supermarkets and if you are pushed for time, then these will make very good substitutes.

GARLIC BUTTER

3 oz (75 g) softened butter
3 cloves garlic, crushed
a pinch of salt

Work the garlic and salt well into the butter before spreading.

HERB BUTTER

3 oz (75 g) softened butter
1 tablespoon chopped mixed herbs (fresh if possible)
a pinch of salt

Work the herbs and salt into the butter, as above.

ANCHOVY BUTTER

3 oz (75 g) softened butter
$\frac{1}{2}$ tin anchovy fillets

Finely chop or pound the anchovy fillets, then work into the butter.

MEAT

Quantities will depend on the age of the children, but they do seem to eat more out of doors! Have a selection of meats if possible, and allow one item of each per guest. For instance, a good mix would be; one chicken drumstick, one beefburger and 2 sausages or alternatively 2 spare ribs and one lamb chop. If in doubt about quantity, err on the over-generous side – it never seems to get wasted.

BEEFBURGERS

Although you can buy these, home-made ones are much better for the barbecue because, being thicker, they won't dry out. For this reason also we suggest you bind the meat with milk rather than egg, as egg tends to dry out the meat in cooking.

Makes 8

2 lb (900 g) lean chuck steak (or more
  expensive steak if you can afford it)
5 tablespoons fresh breadcrumbs
a little milk
a pinch of salt and pepper
1 onion, finely chopped (optional)

Mince the steak yourself, or ask your butcher to mince it for you. Combine all the ingredients, and shape into eight beefburgers about $\frac{1}{2}$ inch (1 cm) thick. Place on a sheet of foil over the grill and cook until they are brown all over, turning once. Children probably prefer them cooked right through rather than pink in the middle.

CHEESEBURGERS

Turn the beefburgers when one side is cooked and put a slice of cheese on top of each one. This will just be melted when the burger is done.

KEBABS

Allow one kebab per guest. You will need long skewers for kebabs so as not to burn your fingers while cooking them. Choose lamb, pork or turkey and buy half a leg of lamb, a small joint of pork, or a turkey joint, allowing about 6 oz (175 g) boned meat per younger child and 8 oz (225 g) per teenagers and adults. Cut the meat into pieces about $1\frac{1}{2}$ inches (4 cm) square, making sure to remove all sinews. Marinate the meat (see page 68) and then push the meat on to the skewers (the more closely you pack the meat the longer it will take to cook, but it will dry out less and taste better). Grill the kebabs over the barbecue, turning them several times and brushing them with oil or the marinade, until they are nice and brown.

To remove the meat from the skewers put the kebabs on the plate, hold it down firmly with one hand, with a fork in the other, and pull the meat slowly off the skewer with the fork.

You can serve kebabs inside the Greek pitta bread, or inside a piece of long French bread (heat both kinds of bread first). This is a good idea if you are serving large numbers, because you can do away with plates, knives and forks.

Using vegetables alternately with the meat makes it go further, prevents it drying out during cooking, and improves its flavour.

Lamb, Tomato and Mushroom Kebabs

Cut small tomatoes in half, remove stalks from the mushrooms and push on to the skewers, turn and turn about with the meat.

Pork, Pineapple and Frankfurter Kebabs

Use large chunks of pineapple or rings cut into quarters to alternate with the pieces of pork and Frankfurter sausage.

SAUSAGES

These are always popular, but for a change try the following variations. Dip the sausages into milk, and then into flour (best with the skinless variety). The end result is a lovely crisp surface which does not burst. Or wrap a rasher of streaky bacon round each sausage and hold in place with cocktail sticks.

HOTDOGS

8 Frankfurter sausages
8 hotdog rolls

Wrap the Frankfurters in foil making a flat parcel. Cook for about 4 minutes on each side, turning once. Cut each roll lengthways, spread a little tomato or barbecue sauce over one surface, and add the Frankfurters.

SPARE RIBS

These are delicious and not at all expensive.

2 spare ribs per person
barbecue sauce (see page 69)

Cook for about 15 minutes, turning occasionally. Spoon a little of the sauce over each one and continue to cook for another 5–10 minutes. They should be crisp and well browned.

SPICY CHICKEN DRUMSTICKS

Chicken is one of the most popular meats for the barbecue. You can buy packs of frozen chicken drumsticks which are ideal to barbecue, but frozen chicken thighs are very much cheaper. They taste just as good, but they don't look so special, so the choice is yours. We do not suggest cooking whole chicken portions over a barbecue because they take so long that the skin tends to burn while the inside is still pink. It is very important to have them cooked right through. Allow one drumstick or thigh per guest.

2 tablespoons flour
1 teaspoon powdered mustard or curry powder
$\frac{1}{4}$ teaspoon ground ginger
$\frac{1}{4}$ teaspoon ground mace, cinnamon or other spice
a little salt and pepper
8 drumsticks (or thighs)
oil

Combine the flour with the spices and seasoning. Brush each drumstick with oil, and roll each one in the mixture. Cook for 15–20 minutes, turning every 5 minutes and either brushing with oil, or dribbling a little oil over the chicken pieces. Brush with a little barbecue sauce during the last few minutes cooking time.

LAMB CHOPS

Allow one per guest. Buy slightly thicker ones than you would normally. Trim them and leave to marinate overnight. Cook for about 15 minutes, turning them every 5 minutes. They are also good cooked in foil. Prepare beforehand a separate parcel for each one, add a spoonful of marinade, and a little butter. Cook for about 20 minutes, turning once.

VEGETABLES

Hot vegetables make a change from salads, and are very little trouble. You can cook almost any vegetable on a barbecue by wrapping it first in kitchen foil. Make sure you keep the fire up.

BAKED POTATOES

Choose smallish potatoes, as big ones would take too long to cook. Scrub them well, sprinkle on a little salt and wrap each one separately in foil. Cook them in the fire (not on the grid) for about an hour, turning once. When they are done, take them out of the foil, cut them open lengthways and add a knob of butter and some grated cheese. New potatoes also are delicious cooked this way – allow a little less than an hour.

CORN ON THE COB

Defrost if frozen. Spread a little butter on each cob and wrap up well in foil. Cook on the fire (not the grid) for about 25 minutes.

SWEET-CORN RINGS

These are ideal for younger children, if you think they will not eat a whole cob each. Defrost the cobs if frozen. Cut them across making neat rings – you should get about six from each cob. Brush with oil and lay them directly on the barbecue grid. They will cook in 3–4 minutes.

TOMATOES

Season with salt and pepper and wrap whole tomatoes in double foil. Cook for about 10 minutes.

BAKED CARROTS, PEAS, FRENCH BEANS, RUNNER BEANS, ETC.

These may sound unusual but are quite delicious. Use fresh or frozen vegetables. If fresh, cut carrots or runner beans into thin strips. Place vegetables in foil, in as many 8 oz (225 g) packets as you think you'll need, spread plenty of butter (about 1 oz or 25 g) over the vegetables, and add a sprinkling of salt. Wrap them up securely and cook directly in the fire for about 10 minutes. Fresh vegetables may take a little longer.

MUSHROOMS

Wrap whole mushrooms in double foil with a good knob of butter, and salt and pepper. Allow about 15 minutes' cooking time.

VEGETABLE KEBABS

These are ideal on their own for vegetarians, or can be served with the barbecued meat – lamb chops, chicken or whatever. The following quantities will feed eight children.

1 lb (450 g) tomatoes
1 red pepper
1 green pepper
8 oz (225 g) courgettes
8 oz (225 g) mushrooms
1 can pineapple chunks

Cut tomatoes in half, core and de-seed peppers, and cut them into flat pieces. Slice the courgettes. Remove stalks from mushrooms. Thread the vegetables and the cut pineapple on to the kebabs and barbecue for 5–10 minutes, basting occasionally.

PUDDINGS

Hot barbecued fruit is delicious and easy, and makes a change from cold puds. Try serving with ice cream, as the combination of hot and cold is irresistible to children (and grown-ups)!

BAKED BANANAS

These seem to shrink during cooking, so allow two per person for adults. Don't peel the bananas, but wrap them in foil and cook for about 20 minutes on the barbecue. Serve them in their skins with crunchy brown sugar and cream while they are still hot.

BAKED BANANAS AU CHOCOLAT

Split the skin and flesh of each banana lengthways and lay in it a chocolate flake. Wrap up in foil, skin and all, and cook for about 20 minutes on top of the barbecue. Serve in their skins, so that guests can scoop out their own.

TOASTED MARSHMALLOWS

Finish your barbecue with these – children love them. Spear the marshmallows on to a skewer and cook holding them over the grid (but not letting them touch it) for about a minute, turning frequently.

BARBECUED ORANGES

Cut round the orange with a sharp knife, removing all the peel and white pith. Stand each orange on buttered foil and sprinkle with brown sugar. Wrap up well and cook on top of the barbecue for about 15 minutes.

BARBECUED APPLES

Choose nice big apples and remove the core with a sharp knife or apple corer. Put each apple on a double layer of foil, and fill the centre with brown sugar, butter and a mixture of raisins, sultanas, chopped dates, walnuts, glacé cherries, depending on what you have in your store cupboard. Wrap up well, and cook for about half an hour in the fire, or an hour on the grid. Serve with cream or ice cream.

BARBECUED PEACHES

Use fresh peaches if you can – the flavour is so much better. Peel them and cut them in half, removing the stone. Otherwise use tinned peaches. Place one half, flat side up, on a layer of double foil and spread on it a teaspoon of brown sugar and a knob of butter. Lay another half peach flat side down on top and wrap up securely. Cook on top of the barbecue for about 15 minutes.

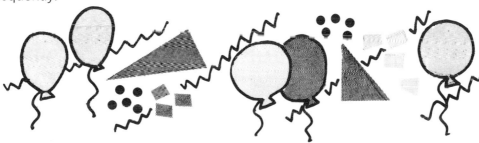

Disco Party Food

The amounts we suggest are for a party of fifty children, but you can easily halve or double the quantities. Always keep portion sizes small.

The Youngest Age Group

If you have any food left over when you've filled the individual plates, keep it back until later on in the evening, so that children can pick at it if they feel peckish.

6 lb (2.7 kg) sausages. You should get roughly thirty-two cocktail sausages per 1 lb (450 g) of weight. Buy either cocktail or chipolata sausages. If using the latter, untwist the skin and squeeze each sausage gently in half, and then retwist – do not cut them apart until they are cooked. Put the sausages on a tray in the oven with a little cooking fat at 350°F, 180°C, Gas Mark 4 for about 30 minutes. Drain off the fat, and leave the sausages to drain on kitchen paper until cool. For this number you will probably find it easier to serve the sausages cold, so cook them the day before the party and put them in the fridge covered with clingfilm once cooled.

50 packets of crisps, Hula Hoops, Monster Munch, etc. If you want a flavoured crisp, try to choose one that is likely to be generally popular, bacon rather than prawn flavour, say.

2–3 lb (1–1.5 kg) salted nuts. Beware: these can provide entertainment if flicked across the room!

50 satsumas. If the party is in the Christmas holiday or term, do try and get a box of these – they are always popular. Leave the children to peel their own.

Mini bridge roll. 25 mini bridge rolls – you will need half for each child. Cut the rolls in half and spread each with the butter – it must be *soft* – filling and a small piece of tomato or cucumber to garnish.

Fillings for mini bridge rolls

9 hard-boiled eggs, finely chopped, mixed with 8 oz (225 g) jar salad cream and some of the soft butter for spreading.

8 large slices of ham – each cut into about 8 pieces with scissors.

Sandwich spread, Marmite, etc.

To decorate mini bridge rolls

8 oz (225 g) firm tomatoes, cut into thin slices and then into smaller pieces.

$\frac{1}{2}$ cucumber cut into thin slices and then into smaller pieces.

Mini bridge roll boats. As above but if you wish to make these into boats you will need also ½ packet (50) cocktail sticks and 2 lettuces. Cut the lettuce leaves into triangular shapes with sides about 3 inches (7.5 cm) long. Use scissors to cut these as it is much quicker than trying to tear the lettuce to shape. Push a cocktail stick through the lettuce in two places to hold the 'sail' upright. Push the end of the stick into the prepared half roll. You can prepare the basic rolls in the morning, and the sails. Clingfilm them separately and refrigerate. Assemble as 'boat' nearer the time of the party.

50 CHEESE STRAW BOATS WITH RICE PAPER SAILS

Oven Temperature: 400°F, 200°C, Gas Mark 6

12 oz (350 g) plain flour, sifted
7 oz (200 g) margarine
4 oz (110 g) Cheddar cheese, finely grated
beaten egg or milk
rice paper cut as triangular sails with 3 inch (7.5 cm) sides
½ packet (50) cocktail sticks

Filling

4 oz (110 g) Cheddar cheese, very finely grated
6 oz (175 g) cream cheese
6 oz (175 g) softened butter

Grease some mini boat-shaped pastry moulds. You will have to bake in batches depending on the number of moulds you have. Make the pastry in a processor, adding enough egg or milk to reach a dough consistency. If you do not have a processor, mix the flour with grated hard margarine until a breadcrumb consistency. Add the cheese. Mix in some egg or milk and knead the dough. Roll out on a floured board and cut boat shapes slightly larger than your mould. Prick the pastry to stop

it rising. Bake for 8–10 minutes until golden brown. Cool slightly and turn on to a wire rack to go cold. You can store these in a tin for a few days.

For the filling, process the ingredients in a food processor or beat very well indeed. Pipe the mixture into your boats. Push a cocktail stick into the top and bottom of the 'sail' and place into the filling to make a 'boat'.

Cheese on sticks. You will need 1 lb (450 g) mild Cheddar cheese and ½ packet (50) cocktail sticks. Sometimes a grocer will cut the cheese for you with his wire, but if not you will need to buy a good square piece of cheese to achieve the best result you can yourself. Cut the piece into slabs about ½ inch (1 cm) thick, and mark out the slab with a knife into squares of about ½ inch (1 cm). Then cut these neatly. Place a cocktail stick into each. Of course you can economise by putting the cubes on a plate without a stick. You could prepare the cubes the day before and clingfilm thoroughly, but don't put the cocktail sticks in until serving.

50 filled mini meringues. You need double quantities of the recipe on page 88, about a 100 little halves and not 50, to allow you to sandwich the two meringue halves together with the cream. Make the meringues very tiny, about 1 inch (2.5 cm) in diameter. You could divide your mixture in half and make one half pink, green or chocolate and the other white, etc. Pipe tiny rosettes on to the Bakewell paper and bake as instructed. When cold, you can store in an airtight tin for up to 2 weeks in advance, and assemble with the cream on the afternoon of the party. Whip 1½ pints (850 ml) double or whipping cream until it is stiff, and sandwich the two halves of the meringues together. Cover with clingfilm.

50 MINI ECLAIRS

Follow the profiterole recipe (see page 97) using a 4-egg mixture. Pipe the pastry with a ½ inch (1 cm) plain nozzle on to the baking sheets, as for the profiteroles. Make 50 eclairs – about 2 inches (5 cm) long – and cook for 15 minutes.

Filling and icing
1 pint (600 ml) double or whipping cream, whipped
3 oz (175 g) cocoa, sieved
1¼ lb (550 g) icing sugar, sieved
¼ pint (150 ml) hot water

When cold fill the eclairs with the whipped cream. Pipe the cream in, using a plain nozzle. Mix the cocoa with a little cold water to make a paste. Add the hot water to the icing sugar a little at a time, then add the cocoa paste and mix. Beat to a soft consistency. Quickly dip the filled eclairs into the chocolate icing and allow to set. Refrigerate or freeze for about a week.

The 'In-Betweens'

50 chicken drumsticks (see page 110).
3 lb (1.4 kg) cocktail sausages (see page 74).
50 packets of crisps (see page 74).

2 large cucumbers. There is no need to peel the cucumbers. Cut them into small sticks, about 3 inches (7.5 cm) long, and really quite thin. Allow three per child. Prepare these in the morning. Clingfilm thoroughly and refrigerate.

1½ lb (675 g) carrots, peeled. Cut into sticks the same size as the cucumber. Allow four per child. Prepare in the morning and either leave in a bowl of cold water or clingfilm thoroughly and refrigerate.

50 ham rolls. 50 soft, and not too large bap rolls; 4 lb (1.8 kg) piece of gammon, cooked until tender and thinly sliced (this will be cheaper than buying ham slices); and 1 lb (450 g) soft butter.

200 cheese squares. 1 lb (450 g) mild Cheddar and 1 lb (450 g) red cheese (Double Gloucester, say). Have contrasting colour cubes (see page 75). Any leftover cheese can be put on the pizza fingers.

50 pizza fingers. 5 Sainsbury's oblong pizzas: add extra topping – grated cheese leftovers (see above), tomato sauce, ham, etc. Cook the pizzas and allow to go cold. Cut them each into approximately twelve pieces.

BREAK-TIME

50 oblong cornets (buy a few extra in case some break), four 1¾ pint (1 litre) long and narrow oblong blocks of Neapolitan ice cream. These blocks should cut into about fifteen slices for the cornets. An optional extra is 50 mini chocolate flakes to stick into the ice cream. If you can't get mini flakes buy the large size and cut each one into three pieces. You will need seventeen of them.

50 individual chocolate mousses (see page 83). Make them in 50 individual paper cups, bowls or saved-up old yoghurt pots, etc. And, unless you have a very large mixing bowl, we suggest you make them in two batches. If you like, pipe a tiny rosette of whipped cream on to each mousse on the afternoon of the party and place a Malteser on top. Do not leave these sitting around – we did and the Maltesers vanished! For fifty mousses, you'll need about 1 pint (575 ml) double or whipping cream and about two 2 oz or 53 g packets of Maltesers.

The Older Group

200 cheese and pineapple cubes on sticks. You will need 1½–2 lb (675–900 g) mild Cheddar cheese, cubed (see page 75). Make the cubes quite small as you will have the pineapple on the sticks as well. Cut the slices from 2 cans of pineapple slices into cubes. Put cheese cube and pineapple cube on to wooden cocktail sticks (you'll need two boxes of 100), and then stick hedgehog-like into two grapefruit.

Pitta bread and pâté. Use 5 pitta bread, 1 large packet of Sainsbury's smooth liver pâté and *soft* butter. Cut the bread into half horizontally, spread with the butter and the pâté. Cut each half into small pieces about 2 × 1 inches (5 × 2.5 cm).

Dips The following is a good tomatoe dip.

12 oz (350 g) fresh cream cheese
4 tablespoons single cream
1½ tablespoons tomato purée or 3 tablespoons
* tomato sauce*
salt and freshly ground black pepper, to taste

Make sure the cream cheese is at room temperature and beat well with the cream and tomato flavouring. Season to taste, and cover with clingfilm.

For a curry dip and a horseradish dip, see page 114, and double the quantities given.

Crudités. Serve Ritz biscuits as well as crudités to dip. You'll need about two packets.

Carrots: 1½ lb (675g)	All cut into 3
Cucumber: 2	inch (7.5 cm)
Cauliflower: 1, cut into florets	sticks (see
Celery: 1 head	page 76)

Pizza fingers (see page 76). Don't have these too large as they will be difficult to handle and the children won't have plates to put them on.

Chocolate praline cake (see page 107, but double the quantities). Allow 1 piece 2 × 1 inches (5 × 2.5 cm) for each child.

4 large packets of crisps (see page 74).
4 boxes twiglets.
100 tiny meringues (see page 75).
200 cocktail sausages (see page 74).

Supper and Dinner Party Food

The quantities we give throughout this section are for eight, but you can easily increase or decrease amounts as required.

Candlelit Dinner

STARTERS

MELON BALLS OR CUBES WITH ORANGE JUICE

1 medium ripe melon (check by pressing your thumb on the top or bottom of the melon – it should give a little)
1 carton fresh orange juice

Cut the melon in half and scoop out the pips. Using a melon baller, scoop the flesh from the melon, or cut the melon in the normal way and chop into small cubes. Place the melon in a bowl and pour on the orange juice. Clingfilm the bowl and refrigerate; or, if you have enough space, divide into the children's bowls, clingfilm each bowl and refrigerate. Take the melon out 30 minutes before you plan to serve the starter so that it will not be too cold for them to eat, and the flavour will be better too. (The children may need a little caster sugar.)

COCKTAIL VOL-AU-VENTS

Oven Temperature: 350°F, 180°C, Gas Mark 4

8 mini vol-au-vent cases
½ pint (275 ml) white sauce

either
1 small cooked chicken breast, chopped, and 2 slices cooked bacon, chopped

or
4 slices of ham, chopped
chopped parsley
chopped lettuce

Cook the vol-au-vents as instructed and leave on the baking tray. Make the white sauce and allow to go cold, covered with clingfilm. Add the cold chicken and bacon – or the ham – to the sauce in the pan and re-cover with clingfilm. Refrigerate. Just before serving put the vol-au-vents on the tray into the pre-heated oven for 2 minutes. Heat the sauce and check the seasoning. Spoon the sauce into the vol-au-vents, sprinkle with parsley and serve on a bed of chopped lettuce to make it look pretty! This allows one vol-au-vent case per person.

MAIN COURSES

SPAGHETTI BOLOGNESE

We do not think that children would eat the usual 2 oz (50 g) per head of dry spaghetti normally suggested on the packets. However, if you think that your guests would eat more, cook 1 lb (450 g) spaghetti.

The Bolognese sauce can be made ahead and frozen or made the day before and refrigerated.

12 oz (350 g) spaghetti (or pasta shells)

Bolognese Sauce
1½ lb (675 g) good lean beef mince
1 large onion, peeled and diced
1 large carrot, peeled and diced
4 oz (110 g) firm button mushrooms, sliced
  (optional, as some children are not keen)
1 heaped tablespoon flour
2 × 15 oz (425 g) cans tomatoes
tomato purée, to taste
a good pinch marjoram
1 dessertspoon redcurrant jelly
salt and freshly ground black pepper
4 oz (110 g) mild Cheddar, very finely grated,
  served separately

Have a large pan of salted water, preheated, so that when you come to bring it to the boil it will not take very long. Cook and drain your spaghetti and toss with some pepper and ground black pepper. Put on a large serving dish and top with the Bolognese.

Fry the mince in a large pan over a moderate heat. (This will release the fat in the meat so that you do not need to cook the vegetables in added oil and make the Bolognese fatty.) When sufficient fat is available, add the onion and cook gently, stirring occasionally, until the onion is softened. Add the carrot and the mushrooms, and fry these gently until softened. Sprinkle in the flour and cook, stirring for a few minutes. Add the canned tomatoes, tomato purée, marjoram, redcurrant jelly and seasoning. Stir, allow the mixture to come to the boil and then cover and simmer gently. You do not want this mixture to be too runny. Cook for about 30 minutes. Ladle the Bolognese on to the spaghetti and serve. Put the bowl of finely grated Cheddar on the table with a teaspoon for the children to help themselves if required.

SHEPHERDS' PIE SPECIAL

This dish could be frozen if made ahead, or made the day before and refrigerated.

Oven Temperature: 350°F, 180°C, Gas Mark 4

1 recipe Bolognese Sauce (see above)
2 lb (900 g) potatoes, peeled and cooked
milk and butter or margarine, to taste
1 egg
4 oz (110 g) mild Cheddar, grated

Make the sauce as directed above. Mash the potatoes with the milk, butter or margarine, and egg, and check the seasoning (you could add a little grated nutmeg to give the potato more flavour if you think the children would like it.) You can either simply spoon the potato on top of the mince, smooth and mark with a fork, or you can put a covering of most of the potato on the mince and reserve some to pipe little rosettes round the edge of the pie. Sprinkle the grated cheese on the pie before putting it in the oven, for 30 minutes.

If this is a birthday treat, just before serving you could put candles in their holders in the piped rosettes as well as putting them in the next course.

CHICKEN PIE

This pie can be made ahead and frozen, or made the day before and refrigerated.

Oven Temperature: 375°F, 190°C, Gas Mark 5

1 × 5–5½ lb (2.25–2.5 kg) chicken
2 carrots, peeled and sliced
2 small onions, peeled, 1 chopped, 1 sliced
bay leaf
6 black peppercorns
2 oz (50 g) butter
4 oz (110 g) mushrooms, sliced (optional, as
  some children are not keen)
2 oz (50 g) flour
salt and freshly ground black pepper
12 oz (350 g) shortcrust pastry
a little milk or beaten egg, to glaze

Cook the chicken by covering it with cold water, adding one of the sliced carrots and the sliced onion, together with the peppercorns and bay leaf. Cover and bring to the boil, then lower the heat and simmer for 1 hour. Allow the chicken to go cool in the stock and then remove.

Fry the finely chopped onion in the butter, and add the remaining sliced carrot. (If you are including the mushrooms, add them briefly when the carrots are softened.) You may need to add a little extra butter here before you add the flour, which should be cooked for a couple of minutes. Remove the pan from the heat. Measure out 1 pint (570 ml) of the stock in which you cooked the chicken – strain it first – no floating bayleaves, please! – and add gradually to the flour and vegetables, stirring well in. Bring this mixture slowly to the boil and cook for a few minutes. Add the seasoning and cool.

Take all the flesh from the cold chicken and cut into bite-sized pieces. Add this to the cold sauce and pour into a pie dish. Grease the edges of the pie dish and roll out the shortcrust pastry. Cut some pastry trimmings to run along the edge of the dish, brush with water and cover the whole pie with the remaining pastry. Press the edges down well, having cut the pastry to fit. Do not put slits in the pie case until you are ready to cook it. Just before you put the pie in the oven, brush with a little milk or beaten egg. Bake for 45–50 minutes.

MOCK MOUSSAKA

Oven Temperature: 375°F, 190°C, Gas Mark 5

1 recipe Bolognese Sauce (see page 79)
2½ lb (1.1 kg) potatoes, peeled and sliced
3 tablespoons cooking oil
8 oz (225 g) mild Cheddar cheese, grated

Sauce
1½ oz (40 g) butter
1 tablespoon flour
½ pint (275 ml) milk
salt and freshly ground black pepper
1 egg, lightly beaten

Make the Bolognese sauce. Fry the potatoes in hot oil for about 10 minutes, making sure that they are cooked through. When they are golden, remove and drain on kitchen paper.

To make the sauce, melt the butter and stir in the flour. Cook gently for a couple of minutes, stirring constantly. Remove from the heat, allow to cool and gradually stir in the milk. Return the pan to the heat and bring the sauce to the boil for a couple of minutes, stirring constantly. Draw off the heat, add the seasoning and then the beaten egg.

Place a layer of the potato slices in a large ovenproof casserole. Add a layer of meat, topped with grated cheese. Continue this layering, leaving some cheese, and top with the sauce, sprinkled with the last of the grated cheese. Bake for 35 minutes until golden.

VEGETABLES

Serve a selection of vegetables – peas, carrots, French beans and so on – but do not mix them up in the serving bowl, as some children may only like one or other of them. However, it can be effective to put rows of two different vegetables into the serving dish.

If you have a canelle knife, cut down the sides of the peeled carrots with the knife, and then slice them across. Each slice of carrot will look a little like a flower.

DUCHESSE POTATOES

Oven Temperature: 400°F, 200°C, Gas Mark 6

3 oz (75 g) butter
1 egg
salt and freshly ground black pepper
2 lb (900 g) potatoes, peeled, boiled and
* mashed*

Add the butter, egg and seasoning to the mashed potatoes, and beat well. Put into a piping bag and pipe rosettes on to a greased baking sheet. Cook for about 25 minutes, near the top of the oven until golden brown.

PUDDINGS

If it is a birthday party, you can put candles on the pavlova or the bombe (try the trick ones that relight). You could also stick sparklers in (buy in indoor firework sets from party shops, if it is not firework time), but only light them when you have put the dessert safely on a table or sideboard. Don't walk with it lit in case one falls off. Put the pavlova or bombe on a tray for the same reason.

PAVLOVA WITH CREAM AND FRUIT

As with meringues, silicon paper is vital for unsticking success! The pavlova base can be made beforehand and either stored in a tin or frozen.

Oven Temperature: 350°F, 180°C, Gas Mark 4
***After 5 minutes,* reduce to 250°F, 120°C, Gas Mark $\frac{1}{2}$**

4 egg whites
8 oz (225 g) caster sugar
1 rounded teaspoon cornflour, sieved
1 teaspoon vanilla essence
1 teaspoon white wine vinegar

Filling
$\frac{1}{2}$ pint (275 ml) double cream
fruit in season (halved strawberries,
* raspberries, 2–3 kiwi fruit, thinly sliced)*

Whisk the egg whites until stiff. Add a tablespoon of the caster sugar gradually, as you are beating. When the mixture is nearly stiff, add the rest of the sugar, whisking it in little by little. Then quickly fold in the cornflour, essence and vinegar with a metal spoon. Place a piece of silicon paper on a baking tray, and pour the mixture on to it. Shape it into a round (if you are worried about this, draw on your baking sheet a large 12 inch/30 cm circle, then turn the paper over and use the line to guide you). Slightly hollow the centre of the pavlova. Bake at the higher temperature for 5 minutes, and then lower the heat and bake for a further hour. Turn your oven off, and leave the pavlova in it to go cold.

Whip the double cream quite stiffly, and spread over the cold pavlova. Arrange your fruit in circles on top.

SNOW PRINCESS CAKE
Oven Temperature: 450°F, 230°C, Gas Mark 8

*1 × 7 inch (18 cm) diameter single layer round
    sponge cake (see Match Cake, page 108)
5 egg whites
10 oz (275 g) caster sugar
1¾ pints (1 litre) Italiano Ice Cream (round)
cheap plastic doll, suitable size, and foil for her
    bodice (remove her legs)
sugar flowers
candles and holders (if a birthday celebration)*

Make a 2-egg simple sponge cake. When the
cake is completely cold, whisk the egg whites
until stiff. Add half the caster sugar and whisk
this mixture again until stiff. Fold in the
remaining sugar with metal spoon. Place the
round-shaped ice cream on top of your sponge
cake, and either spoon the meringue mixture
to cover the ice cream, or pipe it around the
ice cream, using a large star vegetable nozzle.
Decorate the top with meringue rosettes, if you
wish. It is vital to *completely* enclose the ice
cream within the meringue mixture.

   Put the Princess's 'skirt' in a pre-heated
oven and leave for approximately 4 minutes.
The meringue should be soft on the inside but
a little crisp on the outside. (If you wish, you
can freeze the skirt at this point. When you
wish to serve you will need to remove it 30
minutes beforehand, and keep in the
refrigerator.) Just before serving the Princess,
position the top half of the doll (use a piece
of foil as her bodice) on top of the meringue.
Camouflage the join with sugar flowers. If the
doll you use has a hollow body with a 'waist'
the same size as the top of a skewer, you could
secure her by putting the skewer in her body
and placing the pointed end into the meringue
and ice cream. Put candles around her waist.

ICE CREAM BOMBE
*1 pint (575 ml) strawberry soft-scoop ice
    cream
1 pint (575 ml) chocolate ice cream
hundreds and thousands, or chocolate
    vermicelli, to decorate*

Take the strawberry ice cream out of the
freezer for a few minutes to allow it to soften
slightly. Meanwhile prepare a mould: oil the
inside of a 2 pint (1 litre) glass pyrex bowl and
line it with clingfilm. Then spoon the ice cream
into the mould, pressing it well into the base
and up the sides. Make sure there are no gaps
(you will be able to check this through the glass
bowl). Smooth the ice cream into an even layer
about 1 inch (2.5 cm) deep all around the
bowl, then return to the freezer for an hour.
Take the chocolate ice cream out of the freezer
for a few minutes, then scoop it into the centre
of the bowl, again pressing well down. Smooth
the top with a palette knife, cover with clingfilm
and return to the freezer for at least 2 hours.

   It is wise to turn the bombe out in advance
so that you can do it at your leisure. Hold the
bottom of the bowl under hot water very briefly
then invert on to the serving dish, tapping it
sharply. Peel off the clingfilm, and smooth the
creases with a palette knife. Return to the
freezer until you are ready to serve it, and then
decorate.

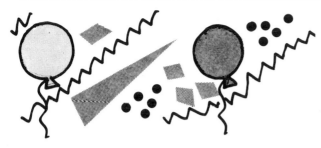

CHOCOLATE MOUSSE

This is a very economical recipe and rather less rich than the usual one. It is also very good for serving in large quantities at disco parties, say.

For 8:
8 oz (225 g) sugar
1 packet (11 g) gelatine
4 heaped tablespoons cocoa
⅓ pint (200 ml) milk
1 large can (14½ fl oz or 413 ml) evaporated milk

For 50 (make in 2 batches):
3 lb (1.4 kg) sugar
5 packets (55 g) gelatine
1 large can (8.82 oz or 250 g) cocoa
1¾ pints (1 litre) milk
3½ large cans (14½ fl oz or 413 ml) evaporated milk.

Stir all the ingredients, except for the evaporated milk, over a low heat until dissolved. Bring to the boil, let it bubble for 1 minute (4 for the larger quantity) then allow to cool slightly. Put the evaporated milk into a mixing bowl and beat until it has increased in volume and is quite solid (this will probably take 3–4 minutes, 6–7 for the larger quantity). Fold in the chocolate mixture, pour the smaller quantities into a serving bowl and put it in the fridge to set. Put the larger quantity into individual pots.

LEMON MOUSSE

A fresh lemony taste and a light texture.

4 oz (110 g) caster sugar
4 eggs, separated
juice of 2 lemons
2 level teaspoons gelatine
¼ pint (150 ml) double cream

Put the sugar, egg yolks and lemon juice into a bowl. Stand the bowl over a pan of hot water which is barely simmering, and whisk until the mixture thickens. Remove from the heat, and whisk occasionally until it is almost cool. Meanwhile, dissolve the gelatine with 2 tablespoons of water in a cup and stand in hot water until the gelatine is dissolved. Pour into the egg and lemon mixture, stirring well. Beat the cream until thick, and stir it in gently. Finally, whisk the egg whites until they hold a peak and fold them into the mixture. Pour into a serving bowl and leave in the fridge until firm.

Pink Party

STARTERS

WILD CHERRY SOUP

1 × 12 oz (350 g) can red cherries
juice of 1 lemon
3 small pots natural unsweetened yoghurt or soured cream
1–2 drops cochineal

Stone the cherries and cut them in quarters. Stir the cherries, cherry juice and lemon juice into the yoghurt. Add the cochineal to improve the colour, if necessary. Chill in the fridge for an hour or two before serving.

PINK PRAWN PÂTÉ

4 oz (110 g) butter
2 tablespoons mayonnaise
4 oz (110 g) cream cheese
1 dessertspoon tomato purée
salt and freshly ground black pepper
1 teaspoon chopped chives
8 oz (225 g) peeled prawns, roughly chopped

The secret of this pâté is to have everything at warm room temperature. Beat the soft butter, add the mayonnaise, then beat in the cream cheese and tomato purée. The mixture should be light and smooth. Add the seasoning, the chives and the prawns. Refrigerate. Remove from the fridge 30 minutes before serving to allow the flavours to develop.

TARAMASALATA

You really do need a food processor to make the best taramasalata.

12 oz (350 g) potatoes, peeled
8 oz (225 g) smoked cods roe
1 small clove garlic, peeled and finely chopped
6 tablespoons olive oil
2 tablespoons lemon juice
freshly ground white pepper
1 heaped teaspoon finely chopped parsley

Boil the potatoes, then allow to cool. Take the skin off the roe using a spoon, and place the roe in the processor with the garlic and potato. Process this mixture and then add the olive oil and lemon juice, very gradually. Blend until well mixed, and add the pepper and parsley. Chill. Serve the taramasalata either with rolls, or hot toast and butter.

PINK TOMATO DIP

8 oz (225 g) cream cheese
2½ tablespoons tomato ketchup

It is important to have your cream cheese at warm room temperature for this to be soft enough to beat well with the tomato ketchup. If you find the consistency is not quite soft enough, add a little oil and vinegar dressing. This must be beaten in very thoroughly. You can make this the day before and refrigerate. Serve with crisps or crudités (try strips of carrot, small cauliflower florets etc).

MAIN COURSES

GAMMON WITH REDCURRANT JELLY SAUCE

Oven Temperature: 350°F, 180°C, Gas Mark 4

2½ lb (1.1 kg) gammon joint
1 carrot, chopped
1 onion, chopped
1 bay leaf
6 peppercorns

Glaze and Sauce
4 tablespoons redcurrant jelly
1 tablespoon white sugar
juice of 1 orange
1 teaspoon ground cinnamon
1 glass red wine
1 oz (25 g) raisins
2 teaspoons arrowroot

Soak the gammon joint in cold water in a large pan for several hours. Pour this water away and add fresh water to just cover the joint. Add the vegetables, bay leaf and peppercorns. Bring the pan to the boil and then simmer gently for 1 hour. Lift joint out and place in roasting tin (retain the cooking liquor). Cut off the rind, and mark the fat with a sharp knife into diagonal lines. Pour several tablespoons of cooking liquor over joint and put in the oven for 30 minutes.

Meanwhile, prepare the glaze. Mix together 1 tablespoon of the redcurrant jelly, the white sugar, orange juice, and ground cinnamon. When the joint has been in the oven for 15 minutes, spoon some of this glaze over the meat, a little at a time. Make the sauce by dissolving the remaining redcurrant jelly in $\frac{1}{2}$ pint (275 ml) of the strained cooking liquor (make sure it's not too salty). Add red wine, raisins and any remaining glaze. Simmer to reduce. Add arrowroot, previously soaked in a little cold water, but do not continue to cook the sauce, or the arrowroot will become thin. Carve the gammon before you serve it and pour a little of the sauce over it; serve the rest of the sauce separately.

CHICKEN WITH PINK MAYONNAISE

This is a simple and delicious recipe, but start cooking the day before you need it, so that the chicken will be completely cold.

Oven Temperature: 350°F, 180°C, Gas Mark 4

1 × 5 lb (2.25 kg) chicken
1 carrot, chopped
1 onion, chopped
1 bay leaf
fresh herbs, or 1 teaspoon dried herbs
salt and freshly ground black pepper
1½ oz (40 g) butter
1½ oz (40 g) flour
1 dessertspoon tomato purée
1–2 drops cochineal
6 tablespoons real mayonnaise
4 oz (100 g) blanched, split almonds (optional)

Put the chicken, chopped carrot, onion, bay leaf, herbs and seasoning into a large lidded ovenproof dish. Add 1 pint (575 ml) water, cover the dish, and cook in the oven for $1\frac{1}{2}$ hours. Leave the chicken in the stock until it is cool, but not cold, then remove to a plate to finish cooling in the fridge. Strain the stock and put in a jug in the fridge for a few hours until the surface fat has solidified. Remove this carefully.

Melt the butter in a pan, and stir in the flour. Cook for a minute then add half the chicken stock. Cook over a low heat until the sauce is thick and smooth, then add the rest of the stock and a little salt and pepper if necessary. Colour the sauce by adding the tomato purée, and a little cochineal. Cover and leave in the fridge. When it is absolutely cold, stir in the mayonnaise.

Remove and discard the chicken skin, and take the meat off the bones. Chop it into bite-sized pieces. Stir into the prepared mayonnaise sauce, spoon on to serving dish, and decorate with the blanched split almonds, arranged in circles.

PINK AND WHITE PASTA SHELLS

1 packet pasta shells or bowknots (not coloured ones)
a few drops of cochineal
oil and vinegar salad dressing

Cook the pasta shells as directed on the packet, but pour into the boiling water several drops of cochineal food colouring. The water will turn a brilliant pink and so will the shells eventually! You may prefer to cook one half of the pasta shells in the pink water, and the other half in plain water. Drain and plunge into cold water. Drain again and toss with oil and vinegar dressing. Allow to go cold, and serve with your chicken.

SIMPLE PINK SALAD SELECTION

8 slices ham
8 slices salami
8 slices any other pink cold meat, pâté, or
  other type of salami

Just roll the ham slices, and arrange on a bed of lettuce together with the selection of other pink meats.

TUNA MOUSSE

You really need a food blender of some sort to make this mousse successfully.

1 × 10 oz (275 g) can tuna fish
¼ pint (150 ml) mayonnaise
1 dessertspoon tomato purée
2 tablespoons water
½ oz (10 g) gelatine
3 tablespoons whipped cream
salt and pepper
1 egg white

White sauce
1½ oz (40 g) butter
1½ oz (40 g) flour
½ pint (275 ml) milk
seasoning

First make the white sauce. Melt the butter, add the flour and cook for a couple of minutes. Remove from the heat and gradually add the milk. Season to taste, and stir over a low heat until the sauce is thick and smooth. Allow to go cold, covered with clingfilm.

Drain the fish and remove any bones. Blend the fish until smooth and add the white sauce, mayonnaise and tomato purée. Put the water in a small bowl, sprinkle the gelatine on it, and allow to soak for 5 minutes. Place the bowl in a little simmering water and dissolve the gelatine. While this cools, fold the whipped cream into the tuna mixture together with any seasoning required. Fold in the dissolved gelatine, whip the egg white until fairly stiff and fold in. Turn at once into a bowl or bowls.

VEGETABLES

PINK MASHED POTATO

2 lb (900 g) potatoes, peeled, boiled and
  mashed
a few drops of cochineal

Simply colour the mashed potato with a few drops of cochineal and beat well to mix the colour in.

You could make this into Duchesse potatoes as on page 81, but reheat in a cool oven so that they don't brown.

RED CABBAGE AND ORANGE

1 oz (25 g) butter
1 small onion, finely chopped
1½–2 lb (700–900 g) red cabbage, finely sliced
¾ pint (425 ml) carton orange juice
1 rounded dessertspoon caster sugar
grated rind of 1 orange

Melt the butter in a pan and gently cook the onion until soft. Add the cabbage and cook, stirring, for a couple of minutes. Pour in ½ pint (275 ml) orange juice and sprinkle on the sugar. Cover and simmer for at least an hour until the cabbage has softened and the juice has almost evaporated (you may need to add extra juice if it boils away too fast).

Just before serving, sprinkle on the orange rind.

RED CABBAGE SALAD

1 small red cabbage, thinly sliced
1 small head of Chinese leaves, thinly sliced
a few radishes, thinly sliced
4 oz (110 g) white button mushrooms, thinly
  sliced
2 small cooked beetroot, peeled and chopped
  into small cubes

Mix up the red cabbage and Chinese leaves and sprinkle the radishes, mushrooms and beetroot on top.

PINK PASTA SALAD

10 oz (275 g) pasta shells
salad dressing
2 red-skinned apples, cubed and tossed in
  lemon juice
½ cucumber, skinned and cubed
sliced radishes
2 sticks celery, sliced

Cook the pasta shells (see page 85) and plunge into cold water, then drain and toss with salad dressing. Make the apple and cucumber cubes a similar but slightly smaller size than the shells. Make sure you toss the apple in lemon juice. Add these and the sliced radishes and celery to the pasta.

PUDDINGS

With any of these puddings, if you are serving cream, whipped or pouring, add some drops of cochineal and before you say 'yuck', remember that this is a joke party!

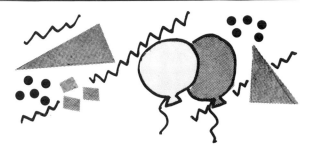

PINK APPLE SNOW

You'll need a large jelly mould – about 2 pints (1 litre) – for this.

3 lb (1.4 kg) cooking apples, peeled, cored and
  sliced
6 oz (175 g) sugar
3 level teaspoons gelatine
6 tablespoons cold water
juice of ½ lemon
a few drops of cochineal
2 egg whites

Put a little water in the bottom of a large pan, and cook the apples gently. Make sure they do not stick as they will go brown. Add a little more water as required. When they are cooked add the sugar and stir until dissolved. Liquidise in a blender or rub through a sieve. Prepare the gelatine by sprinkling it on to the measured cold water in a cup. Stand the cup in a bowl of simmering water until the gelatine is completely dissolved. Add the gelatine, lemon juice and a few drops of the cochineal to the purée (be very careful with the cochineal: the colour to aim for is a soft, not a lurid, pink). Beat the egg whites until stiff, fold gently into the pink purée and pour into the jelly mould. Leave in fridge for 2 3 hours until set. When you are ready to turn the pudding out, run the mould *very quickly* under the hot tap, and invert on to the serving dish, giving it a sharp tap. Serve with pink meringues, sandwiched together with whipped cream.

PINK MERINGUES

Makes about 16 halves
Oven Temperature: 200°F, 100°C, Gas Mark ½

3 egg whites
6 oz (175 g) caster sugar
3–4 drops cochineal
¼ pint (150 ml) double cream

Whip the egg whites until they are stiff, then add half the sugar, and cochineal (be careful). Continue to whip until the mixture is thick and glossy and holds a peak. Fold in the rest of the sugar. If you have a piping bag, pipe rosettes of the mixture on to a baking tray covered with silicon baking paper. If not, use 2 dessertspoons to scoop the mixture on to the paper in neat ovals. Cook at the bottom of the oven for 1½ hours, but keep an eye on them to make sure they do not discolour.

When you are ready to serve, whip the cream and sandwich the meringues together with it.

WHITE MERINGUE WITH STRAWBERRY CREAM

Make the meringues as above, but omit the cochineal. Sandwich them together with this strawberry cream.

¼ pint (150 ml) double cream
3 tablespoons fresh strawberry purée, sieved

Whisk the cream until stiff and fold in the strawberry purée. Add a few drops of cochineal to the cream if you want a stronger pink.

STRAWBERRY ICE CREAM WITH PINK MERINGUES

3½ lb (1.5 kg) strawberries
1 pint (570 ml) double or whipping cream
6 oz (175 g) icing sugar

Keep back 8 oz (225 g) of the best strawberries for decoration. Liquidise the rest in a blender, or press through a sieve. Whip the cream with the sugar until it is thick, and stir into the strawberry purée. Pour into a mould and freeze in the coldest part of the freezer for several hours, preferably overnight. When you are ready to serve the pudding, turn out the mould by running it very quickly under the hot tap, invert on to the serving dish and give the mould a sharp tap. Decorate with the remaining strawberries and serve with a plate of pink meringues, sandwiched together with whipped cream (see above).

RHUBARB FOOL

¾ pint (425 ml) double cream, whipped
1 pint (570 ml) rhubarb purée, sweetened

Whip the double cream until stiff but not too stiff. Fold the purée into the cream, and refrigerate. (If you wanted to jazz up the flavour, grate some orange rind into the rhubarb purée.)

RASPBERRY OR STRAWBERRY SORBET

This can also be served with a lemon sorbet, which looks white. If you have a melon baller, and the time, make a heap of little balls for each person. Decorate with tiny mint leaves.

1 lb (450 g) caster sugar
1 pint (570 ml) water
juice of 2 lemons
1 pint (570 ml) fruit purée

Place the sugar and water in a small heavy-based pan. Dissolve over a low heat, bring to the boil and maintain for a minute. Remove from the heat, stir in the lemon juice and cool. Fold the fruit purée into the cold syrup. Freeze until slushy, beat until smooth, and freeze for a further 2 hours. Beat once more and freeze until firm. Remove from the freezer 20 minutes before serving.

If you want to serve the sorbets in individual wine glasses, frost the rims in pink coloured sugar first (as on page 21).

LEMON SORBET

12 oz (350 g) caster sugar
¾ pint (425 ml) water
juice and finely grated rind of 4 lemons

Place the sugar and water in a small heavy-based pan. Dissolve over a low heat, bring to the boil and maintain for a minute. Remove from the heat, stir in the lemon juice and finely grated rind and allow to cool. Freeze until slushy, beat until smooth, freeze for a further 2 hours, and beat once more. Freeze the sorbet then until it is firm. Remove from the freezer 20 minutes before serving.

Green Party

STARTERS

SPINACH SOUP

This recipe allows for $1\frac{1}{2}$ small ladles of soup per child. You will need a food processor to make this soup.

2 lb (900 g) spinach
4 oz (110 g) butter
1 large onion, finely chopped
3 oz (75 g) flour
2 pints (1.1 litre) milk
salt and freshly ground pepper
¼ pint (150 ml) cream (optional)
nutmeg (optional)

Wash the spinach thoroughly and take off the stalks. Process until finely chopped. You will need to do this in several goes. Melt the butter in a pan and fry the onion gently until it has softened. Add the spinach and cook for a few minutes. Stir in the flour, and cook, stirring constantly. Remove from the heat, and gradually add the milk. Return to the heat, stirring frequently, then bring the soup to the boil. Season to taste.

This soup can be made the day before the party and refrigerated. Reheat and, just before serving, decorate each portion with a swirl of cream and a grating of nutmeg if you wish. Some tiny croûtons (see page 99) add a touch of colour and dash.

WATERCRESS SOUP

Make this as in the above recipe, but substitute 3 bunches of watercress for the spinach. Decorate with tiny sprigs of watercress.

AVOCADO AND ORANGES WITH GREEN HERB DRESSING

4 oranges
3 ripe avocado pears
juice of 1 lemon
chopped parsley and chives
salad dressing

Cut the peel and pith off the oranges with a very sharp knife. Hold the orange over a bowl between your first finger and thumb, and cut each segment, leaving behind the membrane. Collect all the segments in the bowl with the juice. Peel the avocados and cut from top to bottom in thin slices. (Whether you do this with the pear left whole, or whether you remove the stone and cut the slices from the half pear, rather depends on the ripeness of the fruit.) Paint each slice of avocado with the lemon juice using a pastry brush (to stop it going black). Arrange each individual plate with alternative slices of avocado and orange. Mix the chopped herbs in with the salad dressing and pour a little over the fruit.

EGGS WITH GREEN MAYONNAISE OR SALAD CREAM

a bunch of watercress or lettuce leaves
8 hard-boiled eggs, peeled and halved
very finely chopped parsley and chives
½ pint (275 ml) mayonnaise or salad cream

Arrange a little bed of watercress or lettuce leaves on individual plates and place a halved hard-boiled egg on top of each. Mix the herbs in with your mayonnaise or salad cream and pour over. Place a small sprig of watercress on top of the eggs.

STARTER ACCOMPANIMENTS

BROWN BREAD AND GREEN BUTTER PINWHEELS

Thinly slice brown bread and cut off the crusts. Soften some butter and add enough finely chopped parsley to turn the butter green. Spread on the bread slices and roll the slice of bread up. Leave wrapped in damp greaseproof paper in the fridge. Just before serving slice these little rolls into pinwheels – they will look like mini slices of Swiss roll.

HEART-SHAPED BREAD WITH GREEN BUTTER

This can be a bit wasteful, but is a fun way of serving bread and butter. Spread your thinly sliced crustless bread with the green herb butter as above, and cut using a heart-shaped pastry cutter.

HOT FRENCH STICK WITH GREEN HERB BUTTER

Mix softened butter with either chopped fresh mixed green herbs or a little of the mixed herb purée which can be bought from any good supermarket. Carefully cut the French stick into slices (about 1 inch or 2.5 cm thick), but do not cut right through the bottom of the loaf. Spread between each slice with plenty of the butter mixture and, if you have any left over, then spread this over the top of the loaf. Wrap the bread in foil, and bake for about 10 minutes at 425°F, 220°C, Gas Mark 7, then open up the foil and brown and crisp the bread for a further 5 minutes, at 400°F, 200°C, Gas mark 6.

ROLLS OR FRENCH STICK WITH GREEN BUTTER

Just have rolls or French stick cut into slices on the table, and serve them with green butter. Make balls of butter and roll them in finely chopped parsley, or simply press finely chopped parsley all over a slab of butter.

MAIN COURSES

GREEN TAGLIATELLI WITH HAM AND CHICKEN CREAM SAUCE

2 oz (50 g) butter
1 large onion, finely chopped
8 oz (225 g) ham, cut into thin strips
8 oz (225 g) cooked chicken, cut into thin strips
½ pint (275 ml) single cream
salt and freshly ground black pepper
1¼–1½ lb (550–675 g) tagliatelli or any green pasta
4 oz (110 g) Cheddar cheese, finely grated
1 oz (25 g) Parmesan cheese, grated

Make the sauce first. Melt half the butter in a pan and cook the onion gently until soft. Add the ham and the chicken strips and heat through. Stir in the cream and some salt and pepper to taste.

Boil the pasta in a large pan of salted water for about 10 minutes: it should be tender, but not soft. Drain well and toss with the remaining butter. Mix the warm sauce with the pasta and the Cheddar cheese. Toss this mixture and, just before serving, sprinkle the Parmesan on top.

COLD CHICKEN WITH WATERCRESS SAUCE

You will need a processor for this recipe.

5½ lb (2.5 kg) roasting chicken
1 large onion, quartered
1 carrot, peeled and sliced
1 bay leaf
a blade of mace
8 peppercorns
a pinch of salt

Watercress sauce
2 bunches of watercress
½ pint (275 ml) cream
2 tablespoons mayonnaise
2 tablespoons lemon juice
salt

Cover the chicken with cold water in a large pan, and add the other ingredients. Bring to the boil and simmer gently for 1½ hours. Allow the chicken to go completely cold in the liquid before removing. Carve the flesh from the chicken and arrange on a serving dish. Clingfilm and refrigerate until the party.

To make the sauce, reserve a few sprigs of watercress for decoration and process the rest – a little at a time. Lightly whip the cream and add the mayonnaise, lemon juice and salt. Stir this in with the watercress, cover with clingfilm and refrigerate.

To serve, pour some of the sauce over the chicken in the centre of the serving dish. Offer the remaining sauce separately, and decorate the serving dish with the reserved watercress sprigs.

SPINACH AND HAM PANCAKES

Oven Temperature: 350°F, 180°C, Gas Mark 4

We suggest an average of 1½ pancakes per child, thus the pancake batter is for 12 pancakes.

Pancakes

4 oz (110 g) plain flour
a good pinch of salt
1 egg
½ pint (275 ml) milk
a little lard for frying

Filling

1 lb (450 g) frozen spinach
1½ oz (40 g) butter
1 large onion, finely chopped
1½ oz (40 g) plain flour
juice of ½ lemon
½ pint (275 ml) double cream
freshly grated nutmeg
salt and freshly ground black pepper
12 slices ham

Toppings

either
4 oz (110 g) Cheddar cheese, finely grated
or
¾ pint (425 ml) Cheese Sauce (see page 100)

To make the pancakes, sieve the flour into a bowl with the salt, and make a well in the centre. Put in the egg and half the milk. Start to mix in gently, from the well outwards, with a wooden spoon. When all the flour has been mixed in, add the remaining milk gradually, beating continuously. Allow the batter to stand for at least half an hour before you make your pancakes.

Heat a little lard in a frying pan or on a griddle – it should be very hot before you pour any batter in. Coat the bottom of the pan with batter and swivel the pan. Cook until set and brown on the bottom, then turn over to brown the other side. Continue until all the batter is used up.

To make the filling, cook the spinach according to the packet directions. Melt the butter in another pan, and fry the onion gently until soft. Stir in the flour and cook for a little while. Take off the heat, add the lemon juice to the cream and pour this, together with the spinach, into the pan. Mix together and cook over a low heat. Season to taste with nutmeg, salt and pepper.

If you are making the pancakes well before the party, allow the mixture to go cold. Lay out your pancakes with a slice of ham on each, and divide the spinach mixture between them. Roll the pancakes up and put them in a buttered dish (freeze now if liked). Top with chosen topping and warm through in the oven for 15–20 minutes.

VEGETABLES

A green salad could include kiwi fruit, apple, sliced courgettes, watercress, green celery and pepper etc.

Hot green vegetables could include broccoli, peas, beans, spinach (not with the pancakes) and new potatoes with masses of chopped parsley.

ANNA'S GREEN DUCHESSE POTATOES

1 × 8 oz (225 g) packet chopped frozen
  spinach
2 lb (900 g) potatoes, peeled, cooked and
  mashed with butter and milk (page 81)
a pinch of nutmeg

Cook the spinach as instructed on the packet, and evaporate as much water as possible. Beat into the duchesse potato mix with the nutmeg. Pipe into a dish – allow one to two rosettes per child. Prepare these beforehand and heat them up gently.

PUDDINGS

MERINGUE WITH APPLE CREAM FILLING

You can have the meringue white or green, whichever you prefer.

Oven Temperature: 275°F, 140°C, Gas Mark I

4 egg whites
8 oz (225 g) caster sugar
green food colouring
4 tablespoons sweetened apple purée
½ pint (275 ml) double cream, or ¾ pint (425 ml)
  if decorating the top with rosettes

You will need two baking sheets each covered with silicon paper. Draw a 10 inch (25 cm) circle on each piece of paper and turn the paper over.

Whisk the egg whites until they are stiff, but not dry, and add half the sugar. If you are colouring your meringue green add the few drops of food colouring now. Continue to whip until the mixture is thick and glossy and holds

a peak. Fold in the rest of the sugar. Divide the meringue equally between the two circles: either spread it with a palette knife or pipe it if you prefer. Bake at the bottom of the oven for 1–1½ hours, or until it is dry. Check occasionally that it is not browning. Carefully peel off the paper when the meringue is cold.

Make sure the fruit purée is quite solid, not runny. Whip the smaller quantity of cream, and fold in the apple purée. If you feel the colour is not strong enough add a few drops of green food colouring. Spread the cream on one of the meringue layers, and press the other half on lightly. If you have the extra amount of cream, whip this and decorate your meringue with rosettes just before the party.

KIWI FRUIT SORBET

12 oz (350 g) caster sugar
¾ pint (425 ml) water
6 kiwi fruit
¼ pint (150 ml) white wine
a few drops of green food colouring

You will need a food processor to make this sorbet. Make a syrup with the sugar and water as for Lemon Sorbet on page 89. Purée the kiwis with the wine: the little black seeds show up in the purée, and it looks rather pretty. Add a few drops of green food colouring. Mix the purée with the syrup and then continue as on page 89. Serve the sorbet in individual wine glasses, frosted with green sugar first (as on page 21).

APPLE SORBET

12 oz (350 g) caster sugar
¾ pint (425 ml) water
¾ pint (425 ml) thick apple purée
  (unsweetened)
a few drops of green food colouring

Using the apple purée, make as for the Lemon Sorbet on page 89. Serve the sorbet in individual wine glasses frosted with green sugar first (as on page 21)

GOOSEBERRY FOOL

2 lb (900 g) gooseberries
12 oz (350 g) sugar
6 fl. oz (175 ml) water
½ pint (275 ml) cold custard (use packet
  custard)
¼ pint (150 ml) double cream
a few drops of green food colouring, if
  necessary

Optional garnish
¼ pint (150 ml) double cream, whipped

Prepare the gooseberries and cook them with the sugar and water until they are very soft. Sieve them or process in a food mixer. Process or mix with the custard. Whip the cream to soft peak consistency and fold this into the fool. (If you feel the fool does not look green enough, add a few drops of green food colouring.) Pour the mixture into a glass bowl or divide between eight glasses. Cover with clingfilm and chill. Decorate with extra whipped cream rosettes, if you like.

GREEN AND WHITE FRUIT SALAD

It is most important to choose apples and pears with green skins and white flesh, and a melon with greenish coloured flesh.

4 oz (110 g) sugar
¼ pint (150 ml) water
juice of 2 lemons
2 green apples, cored and sliced
1 green melon, halved and scooped or sliced
8 oz (225 g) green seedless grapes
3 kiwi fruit, peeled and sliced
1 can lychees, drained
2 white pears, cored and sliced
2 bananas (optional)

Put the sugar and water in a small pan over a low heat, and when the sugar has quite dissolved, bring to the boil and simmer gently for 5 minutes. Add the lemon juice to the syrup, and cool. Combine all the fruit except the bananas in a bowl and pour the syrup over. Leave it for at least an hour before serving. Peel and slice the bananas and stir them into the rest of the fruit at the last minute.

CHEESE

If the children are older and if you think that they would appreciate a cheese board to precede or follow the dessert, then include on this Sage Derbyshire Cheese and Herb Roulé. Serve with as green a celery as you can find. (If you are doing a green and white party serve Bath Oliver Cheese Biscuits which are practically white.) Decorate the board with green watercress, parsley or green grapes.

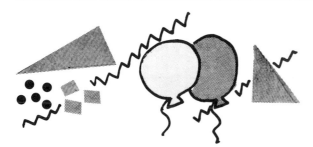

Black and White Buffet Supper

STARTERS TO SERVE WITH DRINKS

CURRY DIP

6 oz (175 g) fresh cream cheese
2 tablespoons single cream
curry paste or powder to taste
salt and freshly ground pepper, to taste

Make sure the cream cheese is at room temperature and beat well with the cream and curry powder. Season to taste. Cover with clingfilm. Serve with cauliflower florets cut to manageable size, and sliced mushrooms (try to find some with a good dark inside).

HORSERADISH DIP

6 oz (175 g) fresh cream cheese
2 tablespoons single cream
1½ tablespoons horseradish sauce, or to taste
a few drops of Worcestershire sauce (optional)
salt and freshly ground pepper, to taste

Mix and serve as above.

PRUNES STUFFED WITH CREAM CHEESE

8 oz (225 g) cream cheese
salt and fresh ground pepper
1 packet of Sainsbury's ready prepared,
ready to eat (really scrumptious) prunes

Have the cream cheese at room temperature and mix with the seasoning. Cut the prunes open and stuff them with the cream cheese.

CELERY STICKS WITH STILTON AND CREAM CHEESE FILLING

a few sticks of crisp celery, washed well
4 oz (110 g) cream cheese
4 oz (110 g) Stilton cheese
1 tablespoon single cream
freshly ground pepper

Have the cheeses at room temperature and blend them together until smooth with the single cream. Either pipe or spoon the mixture into the hollow of the celery sticks. Cut the sticks into 1 inch (2.5 cm) long pieces and season with pepper.

BLACK GRAPES STUFFED WITH CREAM CHEESE AND WALNUTS

8 oz (225 g) black grapes
4 oz (110 g) cream cheese
1 oz (25 g) finely chopped walnuts
salt and freshly ground pepper

Remove the pips from the grapes without cutting the grapes completely in half. Have the cream cheese at room temperature and thoroughly mix with the finely chopped walnuts and seasoning. Put a little of the stuffing into each grape.

BUFFET SELECTION

CHICKEN SALAD WITH BLACK GRAPES OR CHERRIES

4 lb (1.8 kg) cooked chicken
½ pint (275 ml) natural yoghurt
½ pint (275 ml) mayonnaise
2 tablespoons single cream
½ cucumber, peeled and chopped
2 apples, peeled, cored, chopped and
   sprinkled with lemon juice
3 sticks celery, chopped
8 oz (225 g) black grapes, pipped, or black
   cherries, stoned
salt and freshly ground pepper

Cut the flesh of the chicken into bite-sized pieces. Combine the yoghurt, mayonnaise and cream in a large bowl and add the fruit and vegetables and the chicken flesh. Season to taste, and chill in the fridge.

WHITE RICE SALAD WITH RAISINS AND ALMONDS

¼ pint (150 ml) French dressing
1 lb (450 g) cooked rice (use white long-grain
   not brown)
4 oz (110 g) raisins
4 oz (110 g) flaked almonds, toasted
2 sticks celery, chopped
freshly ground black pepper

Add the salad dressing to the rice while it is still hot, and mix thoroughly. Allow this to cool, then add the raisins, almonds, celery and freshly ground pepper.

EGG SALAD WITH MOCK CAVIAR

8 hard-boiled eggs, peeled and halved
   lengthways
lettuce
6 tablespoons mayonnaise
1 small jar lumpfish roe (mock caviar)

Arrange the eggs on a bed of lettuce on individual plates. Spoon a little mayonnaise on top of each, and decorate with some of the mock caviar.

CHINESE LEAF SALAD

1 head of Chinese leaves
1 head of chicory
4 oz (110 g) mushrooms, sliced (choose
   mushrooms which have a good contrasting
   white and dark brown inside)
1 bulb of fennel, sliced thinly
8 oz (225 g) black olives
salad dressing

Slice the Chinese leaves and put in the salad bowl. Place leaves of chicory upright around the edge of the bowl. Scatter the remaining ingredients on top.

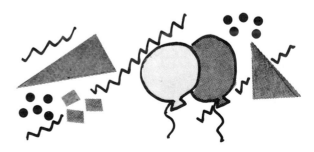

PUDDINGS

PROFITEROLES AND DARK CHOCOLATE SAUCE

You could also make eclairs, large or small, with this choux pastry mixture. Simply pipe a line instead of a walnut, to whatever length or thickness you desire.

Makes 24

Oven Temperature: 400°F, 200°C, Gas Mark 6

2½ oz (65 g) plain flour
a pinch of salt
2 oz (50 g) butter
¼ pint (150 ml) water
2 eggs (size 2)

Chocolate sauce
5 oz (150 g) sugar
3–4 tablespoons golden syrup
2 oz (50 g) cocoa powder
½ teaspoon vanilla essence
3 oz (75 g) butter
7 fl oz (200 ml) water

Filling
¾ pint (425 ml) double cream

Sieve the flour and salt together. Put the butter and water in a heavy-based pan, and heat gently until the butter has melted. Bring to the boil, and tip in the flour and salt, beating until the mixture comes together and leaves the sides of the pan. Remove from the heat and allow to cool for 2–3 minutes. Beat in the eggs, one at a time, beating well until the mixture has taken up the egg before adding any more.

Place a large star nozzle in a piping bag and fill with the pastry mixture. Lightly dampen a baking tray. Pipe the mixture in small mounds about the size of a walnut. Bake for 20–25 minutes, and you must *not* open the oven door during cooking. Remove from the oven and make a small hole in the side of each profiterole. Return to the oven for 5 minutes. Remove again and cool on a wire rack.

To make the sauce, heat all the ingredients together over a gentle heat, stirring it. Bring the sauce to the boil and keep boiling for approximately 3–4 minutes. Leave to cool.

Whip the cream until stiff and put in a piping bag. Cut the cold profiteroles open on one side and pipe in the cream. Pile on to a dish and, just before serving, pour over the cold chocolate sauce.

LEMON SYLLABUB WITH BLACK CHERRIES

1 × 12 oz (350 g) can stoned black cherries (not red) or 12 oz (350 g) fresh black cherries, stoned
¾ pint (425 ml) double cream
juice and finely grated rind of 3 lemons
3 oz (75 g) caster sugar
¼ pint (150 ml) white wine

Strain the canned cherries of juice if you are using them and drain on kitchen paper. Divide the cherries between eight glasses. Whip the cream until soft and starting to thicken, then gradually add the juice and the rind of the lemons, together with the sugar and white wine. Continue whipping until the mixture is fairly thick. Pour the mixture over the cherries, and chill.

CHOCOLATE ROULADE

Oven Temperature: 350°F, 180°C, Gas Mark 4

6 eggs, separated
6 oz (175 g) caster sugar
2 oz (50 g) cocoa
icing sugar

Filling

8 oz (225 g) plain chocolate, broken up
2 tablespoons water
2 eggs, separated
¼ pint (150 ml) double cream, whipped

To make the roulade, put the egg yolks and caster sugar into a bowl. Whisk until the mixture thickens. Add the cocoa and gently mix it in. Whisk the egg whites until stiff and then carefully fold into the chocolate mixture. Pour the mixture into a tin 12 × 7 inches (30 × 18 cm) which you have previously lined carefully with greaseproof paper. Cook for about 20 minutes until it has risen and is springy to the touch. Leave to cool (and incidentally to shrink somewhat).

To make the filling, put the chocolate pieces into a bowl with the water and melt over a pan of hot water. Beat it a bit to make sure it is smooth. Beat the yolks into the chocolate mixture. Whisk the egg whites and fold them in as well. Leave to cool.

To prepare the roulade, turn it on to a piece of greaseproof paper which you have sprinkled with icing sugar. Remove the paper from the bottom of the cake and spread it first with the cool chocolate filling, and then with the whipped cream. Roll up the cake into a log, and however gently you do this, you will probably get some cracks in the cake surface: this adds to its log-like look!

YOGHURT CREAM SURPRISE

½ pint (275 ml) double cream
½ pint (275 ml) natural yoghurt
dark soft brown sugar
fruit (optional)

Whip the cream until soft and thick, and stir in the yoghurt. If you want to add fruit – black grapes, for instance – put them at the bottom of a glass bowl. Pour the yoghurt and cream mixture on top and cover to a depth of about ½ inch (1 cm) with the soft brown sugar. This must be done 24 hours before you intend to serve the pudding as then the topping becomes almost as crisp as if it had been grilled. The colour contrast is much better after 24 hours and although it is a dark brown, the contrast between the white bottom showing through the glass bowl and the dark top would be effective for this party.

BLACKCURRANT/BLACKBERRY SORBET AND LEMON SORBET

Make up the Lemon Sorbet as on page 89, and make a 'black' sorbet with a purée of either blackcurrants or blackberries and a sugar syrup. Follow the Lemon Sorbet recipe thereafter. Serve a scoop of black and of white per guest.

CHEESE

There are lots of black and white cheeses: Chèvre Blanc (white goat's cheese); Tomme aux Raisins (white cream cheese rolled in black grape seeds); Rambol au Poivre (cream cheese with black peppers); or Brie. Serve with Bath Oliver biscuits or black rye bread, and white celery.

A selection of food and drink.

The Pink Party (see page 22).

Mixed Dinner Parties

SUMMER MENU

CHILLED CUCUMBER SOUP

You will need a food processor or blender to make this soup. If it is a very cold night you could always heat this soup up and serve it with hot bread rolls or croûtons.

3 cucumbers
2 pints (1.1 litre) milk
3 oz (75 g) butter
1 large onion, finely chopped
3 oz (75 g) flour
1 pint (570 ml) good well flavoured chicken
  stock (or use a cube and add a bay leaf)
a couple of drops of food colouring (if required)
finely chopped mint, parsley or chives
¼ pint (150 ml) single cream

Cut off eight thin slices of cucumber, unpeeled. Peel the remaining cucumber and take out the seeds. Chop and process or blend with a little milk.

Melt the butter in a pan, add the onion and allow to cook gently until softened. Add the flour and cook for a few minutes, then add the cucumber purée. Mix thoroughly, and pour in the remaining milk and the stock. Bring to the boil and allow to cook for a few minutes. Pour the soup into a bowl and allow to cool. Cover and chill until you wish to serve it.

If you feel the colour is rather brown (this will depend on the stock you have used) add a couple of drops of green food colouring. Just before serving add chopped herbs, a swirl of cream and a slice of cucumber on the top.

CROÛTONS

6 slices white bread
½ pint (275 ml) cooking oil

Trim the crusts off the bread and cut into neat ½ inch (1 cm) squares. Heat the cooking oil in a frying pan and drop in one croûton to test the heat. It should sizzle, but not turn brown too quickly. Take it out and put all the others in, turning them after half a minute until they are golden brown all over. Watch them carefully because they can go too brown very quickly. Take them out and drain them on kitchen paper. Serve hot. You can make these in advance and reheat them when you need them.

CHERRY CHICKEN SALAD

5 lb (2.25 g) chicken, cooked with tarragon
1 lb (450 g) cherries
¼ pint (150 ml) double cream
½ pint (275 ml) mayonnaise
2 tablespoons tarragon vinegar
salt and freshly ground pepper
finely chopped parsley

Cut the chicken flesh into bite-sized pieces. Stone the cherries and leave them on kitchen paper to drain off juice while you prepare the sauce. (If you can get hold of a garlic press with a cherry stoner incorporated in the handle, these are excellent for the job.) Whip the cream lightly to a soft peak texture and mix with the mayonnaise and vinegar. If you feel you can't taste a sufficient tarragon flavour, add more vinegar here. Fold in the chicken and cherries and check the seasoning. Sprinkle with chopped parsley before serving. We suggest you make a rice and a green salad to serve with the chicken, but if it is a cold night you could bake some potatoes.

WINTER MENU

HADDOCK MOUSSE WITH HEART-SHAPED BREAD AND BUTTER

Cut the bread and butter into heart shapes as described on page 90 – or serve with rolls.

1 lb (450 g) smoked haddock fillet
4 peppercorns
a piece of onion
some parsley
bay leaf
1 pint (570 ml) cold water
½ oz (15 g) gelatine
½ lemon
½ pint (275 ml) double cream, lightly whipped
freshly ground pepper
chopped parsley

Place the haddock, peppercorns, onion, parsley, bay leaf and water in a pan and bring to the boil. Cover and allow to simmer for 5 minutes and then remove from the heat. Leave the haddock in the stock until it is cool. Drain and flake the flesh. Retain the stock.

Strain ½ pint (275 ml) fish stock into a small bowl, and sprinkle on the gelatine. Leave this to soak for 5 minutes. Place the bowl over a pan of hot water and allow the gelatine to dissolve. Cool the stock and when it begins to thicken, fold in the haddock, lemon juice and lightly whipped cream. Check the seasoning and divide the mixture between eight ramekin dishes. Cover with clingfilm, and chill. Before serving, sprinkle with chopped parsley.

LASAGNE

Oven Temperature: 350°F, 180°C, Gas Mark 4

12 oz (350 g) lasagne

Meat sauce
1 tablespoon oil
1 large onion, finely chopped
2 slices streaky bacon, chopped
1½ lb (675 g) lean beef, minced
8 oz (225 g) button mushrooms, thinly sliced
2 tablespoons flour
2 tablespoons tomato purée
1 tablespoon redcurrant jelly
1 × 15 oz (425 g) can tomatoes
1 carrot, thinly sliced
1 teaspoon mixed herbs (amount depends on children's taste)
salt and freshly ground black pepper
½ pint (275 ml) stock

Cheese sauce
2 oz (50 g) butter
2 oz (50 g) plain flour
1 pint (570 ml) milk
8 oz (225 g) Cheddar cheese, finely grated
2 oz (50 g) Parmesan cheese, grated, or extra grated Cheddar

Many people find it easiest to make the lasagne using the pasta which does not need any preliminary cooking. In this case, we suggest that you make an extra ½ pint (275 ml) of cheese sauce. However, if you prefer to boil the lasagne first – for about 15–20 minutes – the non-stick secret is not to drain the water off the lasagne, but, using two fish slices, take the pasta from the water just as you are assembling the dish. Just shake the excess water off, and you will find the pasta much easier to deal with.

To make the meat sauce, heat the oil in a large pan and fry the onion gently, until soft.

Add the bacon and fry a little before adding the mince. Turn the mince until it is brown, then add the mushrooms, and continue cooking for a couple of minutes. Then add the flour, tomato purée and redcurrant jelly, and stir well. Add the canned tomatoes, carrot, herbs, seasoning and stock, and bring to the boil. Allow to simmer for 45 minutes, and remember to stir occasionally.

To make the cheese sauce, melt the butter in a pan and stir in the flour. Cook gently for a couple of minutes. Take off the heat and gradually add the milk. Return to the heat, and bring to the boil until the sauce has thickened. (If your sauce is lumpy use a wire whisk to get rid of the lumps.) Add some salt and pepper and stir in the Cheddar cheese.

Grease a $5\frac{1}{4}$ pint (3 litre) dish. If you haven't got one large enough, simply divide the lasagne between two smaller greased dishes. Put a third of the meat sauce, topped by the cheese sauce and followed by half the lasagne into the dish or dishes. Repeat the layers and finish with the grated Parmesan on top. Bake in the oven for about 45 minutes until the top is nicely browned. This dish can either be made the day before, or it freezes extremely well. Allow the lasagne to defrost overnight and then reheat.

For an optional topping, you can sprinkle the lasagne with 2 oz (50 g) finely grated Cheddar cheese, topped by 1 oz (25 g) of breadcrumbs and 2 oz (50 g) of chopped almonds. This may sound strange, but the nuts give a lovely crunchy contrast to the rest of the dish. And for a sauce alternative, you could add a $\frac{1}{5}$ teaspoon of mustard to the cheese sauce, when you add the seasoning and cheese.

FRUIT FONDUE

Don't serve this after a meat fondue!

10 oz (275 g) plain chocolate
3 tablespoons orange juice
2 tablespoons cream (optional)
Selection of sliced or diced fresh fruit, eg nectarines, peaches, oranges or satsumas (in segments), kiwi fruit, grapes, half a small pineapple, bananas – don't slice these early – strawberries.

Melt the broken chocolate with the orange juice over a very gentle heat. Do not boil this mixture. Stir constantly until it is quite smooth. Pour it into the fondue pan and keep the mixture warm. Stir in the cream just before serving if you intend to include it.

Have a couple of bowls of mixed prepared fruits at either end of the table. The guests dip whichever fruit they wish on their fondue forks into the sauce.

ICED COFFEE

3 tablespoons instant coffee
sugar to taste (about 2 tablespoons)
$\frac{1}{4}$ pint (150 g) boiling water
2 pints (1.1 litre) cold milk
ice cubes

Put the coffee and sugar in a large jug. Add the boiling water and stir well. Add the cold milk and ice cubes. Keep in the fridge until needed.

Some people might prefer no sugar at all, in which case you might feel it would be safer to omit the sugar and serve caster sugar separately for anyone who wants it (although it won't dissolve so well in the cold coffee).

Match Party Food

The quantities given in this section are for either eight or twenty-four children, unless specified. If you are having more or fewer people adapt the quantities to fit your numbers.

LUNCHES

SAUSAGE MOUSSAKA

Oven Temperature: 375°F, 190°C, Gas Mark 5

For 24:
6 lb (2.7 kg) potatoes
3 onions, very finely chopped
2 oz (50 g) butter
6 lb (2.7 kg) sausages
1 lb (450 g) Cheddar cheese, grated
salt and pepper
½ pint (275 ml) milk

For 8:
2 lb (1.1 kg) potatoes
8 oz (225 g) onions, very finely chopped
1 oz (25 g) butter
2 lb (900 g) sausages
6 oz (175 g) Cheddar cheese, grated
salt and pepper
3 tablespoons milk

Peel the potatoes, and boil them until they are cooked, but still slightly firm. Drain, and when they are cool enough to handle, slice them. Fry the onion in the butter for at least 5 minutes until soft but not brown. Remove the onion, and cook the sausages in the pan for about 10 minutes. Layer the potatoes and sausages in an ovenproof dish (or dishes), adding the cheese and onion to each layer, together with a little seasoning. Pour on the milk and cook for about 20–25 minutes.

Meanwhile, prepare the cheese sauce. Make a roux with the butter and flour, stir in the milk to make a smooth sauce, then add three-quarters of the cheese and a little salt and pepper. When the meat is cooked, drain off any fat if necessary, and transfer to a larger ovenproof dish or dishes. Arrange the sliced potatoes on top of the meat, pour on the cheese sauce, sprinkle the remaining cheese over the top and cook for 30 minutes in the oven until the top is golden and bubbling.

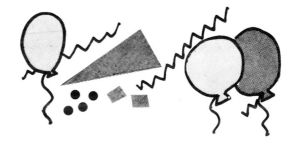

CHEESY MEAT AND POTATO PIE

Oven Temperature: 350°F, 180°C, Gas Mark 4

For 24:

6 lb (2.7 kg) minced meat
3 onions, very finely chopped
1½ pints (850 ml) stock
3 tablespoons tomato purée
salt and pepper
6 lb (2.7 kg) potatoes
6 oz (175 g) butter
6 oz (175 g) flour
2½ pints (1.4 litres) milk
1 lb (450 g) Cheddar cheese, grated

For 8:

2 lb (900 g) minced meat
1 onion, very finely chopped
½ pint (275 ml) stock
1 tablespoon tomato purée
salt and pepper
2 lb (1.1 kg) potatoes
2 oz (50 g) butter
2 oz (50 g) flour
¾ pint (425 ml) milk
6 oz (175 g) Cheddar cheese, grated

Combine the meat and onion in an ovenproof dish or dishes (use best quality minced meat, because there is so much less fat on it). Mix the stock, tomato purée, salt and pepper together and pour over the meat. Cook for 2 hours in the preheated oven, stirring occasionally.

Peel and cook the potatoes, taking them off the heat when they are still firm. Drain and slice them when they are cool enough to handle.

OSLO STEAK STEW

The tangy, slightly spicy flavour of this stew has a great appeal for children.

Oven Temperature: 325°F, 160°C, Gas Mark 3

For 24:

8 lb (3.6 kg) chuck steak, trimmed and cut into
* bite-sized pieces*
cooking oil
8 onions, sliced
3 pints (1.75 litres) stock or water
3 Oxo cubes
3 level tablespoons mild curry powder
3 tablespoons Worcestershire sauce
3 oz (75 g) cornflour
¼ pint (150 ml) vinegar
6 oz (175 g) brown sugar
6 tablespoons tomato purée

For 8:

2½ lb (1.1 kg) chuck steak, trimmed and cut
* into bite-sized pieces*
cooking oil
3 onions, sliced
1 pint (570 ml) stock or water
1 Oxo cube
3 teaspoons mild curry powder
3 teaspoons Worcestershire sauce
2 tablespoons cornflour
3 tablespoons vinegar
3 tablespoons brown sugar
2 tablespoons tomato purée

Fry the meat lightly on both sides in the cooking oil and remove to a casserole dish or dishes. Fry the onion and add to the meat. Mix all the other ingredients and pour into the dish or dishes. Put the lid on and cook in the preheated oven for 2–2½ hours, stirring occasionally.

ICE CREAM AND SAUCES

To serve twenty-four children you will need three large blocks (4 litres) of Neapolitan ice cream cut into portions. For eight children serve one block. We suggest using blocks because they are so much quicker and easier to serve for large numbers. All these sauces can be made in advance and left in a covered saucepan. All you have to do is reheat them just before serving. Add a little milk if the sauce has gone thick.

Mars Bar Sauce

For 24:
*2 packets mini or
12 large Mars Bars
a little milk*

For 8:
*4 large Mars bars
a little milk*

Chop up the Mars Bars and place in a heavy bottomed saucepan with a little milk. Melt over a low heat, stirring constantly. Add a little more milk if the sauce is a bit thick, or to eke it out!

Toblerone Sauce

If you prefer a nutty sauce, substitute Toblerone for the Mars Bars.

Marshmallow Sauce

For 24:
*12 oz (350 g) sugar
6 tablespoons water
2 packets (9 oz/250 g)
 marshmallows
a few drops vanilla
 essence
a few drops cochineal
3 egg whites*

For 8:
*4 oz (110 g) sugar
2 tablespoons water
8 pink marshmallows
a few drops vanilla
 essence
a few drops cochineal
1 egg white*

Dissolve the sugar in the water, bring to the boil and simmer for 5 minutes (8–9 minutes for the larger quantities). Cut up the marshmallows, add them to the sugar syrup and stir them until they have melted. Add the vanilla and cochineal. Whip the egg white stiffly and fold into the marshmallow mixture. Serve warm with the ice cream.

Chocolate Fudge Sauce

For 24:
*1½ pints (850 ml) milk
3 level tablespoons
 cocoa
1 lb 2 oz (500 g) sugar
9 oz (250 g) butter*

For 8:
*½ pint (275 ml) milk
1 level tablespoon cocoa
6 oz (175 g) sugar
3 oz (75 g) butter*

Heat the milk and pour a little over the cocoa in a bowl to make a smooth paste. Add the cocoa paste to the rest of the milk and add the sugar and butter. Stir over a gentle heat in a large heavy-bottomed pan until they are dissolved. Bring to the boil and boil briskly for about 5 minutes – up to 10 minutes for the larger quantity – until the mixture begins to thicken, stirring all the time. If you have a sugar thermometer, boil until it reads 217°F (100°C). Cool slightly before using.

Butterscotch Sauce

For 24:
*12 oz (350 g) light brown sugar
6 oz (175 g) butter
1¼ lb (600 g) golden syrup
¾ pint (425 ml) milk*

For 8:
*3 oz (75 g) light brown sugar
2 oz (50 g) butter
4 large tablespoons golden syrup
¼ pint (150 ml) milk*

Put the sugar, butter and syrup into a saucepan, and stir over a gentle heat until dissolved. Simmer for 3 minutes (5 minutes if you are making the larger quantity), stirring all the time. Take off the heat and slowly add enough milk to make a pouring consistency. Serve hot with the ice cream.

TEAS

BELLA'S CHEESE STRAWS

Makes 30

These puff up beautifully when they cook.

Oven Temperature: 425°F, 220°C, Gas Mark 7

3 oz (75 g) Cheddar cheese
2 oz (50 g) plain flour
1 level teaspoon baking powder
a pinch Cayenne pepper
2 oz (50 g) butter or margarine
2 egg yolks

Grate the cheese into a mixing bowl. Sift the flour, baking powder and Cayenne into the bowl. Cut the butter or margarine into small pieces and rub into the flour until the mixture resembles fine breadcrumbs. Add one of the egg yolks, and mix with a wooden spoon to a stiff dough. Shape the dough into a rectangle approximately 9 × 6 inches (23 × 15 cm) on a floured board. Cut into straws and place on ungreased baking sheet. Brush with the remaining egg yolk. Cook for 8–12 minutes towards the top of the oven until golden brown. Allow to cool on baking sheet.

SAUSAGE ROLLS

Makes 24
Oven Temperature: 350°F, 180°C, Gas Mark 4
After 15 minutes: 325°F, 160°C, Gas Mark 3

15 oz (425 g) packet Jusrol flaky pastry
8 oz (225 g) sausagemeat
a little milk

Make these the day before the party. Roll out the pastry into a rectangle on a floured board, and cut into two strips, lengthways. Divide the sausagemeat into two halves, and roll with your hands into two sausages the same length as the pastry. Brush the long edges of the pastry with milk, and lay the sausagemeat down the length of the pastry. Bring the edges up to the centre to cover the sausagemeat. Press the edges firmly together, making an indented edge with your fingertips and brush the pastry with milk. Place on a greased baking tray and cut into rolls 1½ inches (4 cm) long, and cook for 15 minutes. Reduce the oven temperature, and cook for a further 10 minutes, but do not let them get too brown. They should rise well, and be deep gold to light brown in colour.

CHEESE SCONES

Makes 24

These can be made a day or two before the party, and kept in an airtight tin.

Oven Temperature: 350°F, 180°C, Gas Mark 4

12 oz (350 g) self-raising flour
1 level teaspoon salt
3 oz (75 g) butter
3 oz (75 g) Cheddar cheese, grated
a little milk

Stir the flour and salt together, and rub in the fat, until the mixture resembles fine breadcrumbs. Add the cheese and enough milk to make a stiff dough, but be careful not to make it too slack. Roll it out to a thickness of at least ½ inch (1 cm), or pat it down with your hands, and cut it out into rounds with a 2 inch (5 cm) diameter pastry cutter. Place on a greased baking tray, brush the tops with milk and cook for about 10 minutes. You can cut them in half and spread the halves with butter before serving.

CHOCOLATE SHORTBREAD TREAT

These are at their best when freshly made, but will keep well if necessary.

Makes 24

Oven Temperature: 350°F, 180°C, Gas Mark 4

9 oz (250 g) flour
1½ oz (40 g) caster sugar
6 oz (175 g) butter

Filling

6 oz (175 g) butter
6 oz (175 g) soft brown sugar
3 level tablespoons golden syrup
1½ small cans condensed milk

Icing

12 oz (350 g) plain dessert chocolate
1½ oz (40 g) butter

Grease a baking tin. To make the shortbread base, sift the flour into a bowl, add the sugar and rub in the butter until the mixture resembles fine breadcrumbs. Knead it into a ball and press well into the tin. Cook for 15 minutes. Leave to cool in the tin.

To make the filling, put all the ingredients into a saucepan and stir over a gentle heat until the sugar has dissolved. Bring to the boil and, stirring continuously, boil gently for 7 minutes. Take off the heat and beat well, then pour on to the shortbread base. Allow to cool before adding the icing.

To make the icing, cut the chocolate up roughly and melt over a very gentle heat with the butter. Spread evenly over the filling. When the chocolate is quite cold cut into twenty-four fingers.

CHOCOLATE CRUNCH CAKES

Makes 24

Make two or three days in advance and keep in the fridge.

1 lb (450 g) plain chocolate
2 egg yolks
4 oz (110 g) unsalted peanuts, chopped
4 oz (110 g) Rice Krispies
24 paper cases

Melt the chocolate over a very gentle heat, and stir in the egg yolks. Then stir in the dry ingredients until they are well mixed. Put teaspoonsfuls of the mixture into paper cases and leave to set in the fridge.

NUTTY CHOCOLATE TREAT

Makes 24

These biscuits will freeze or you can make them several days in advance and keep them in the fridge.

8 oz (225 g) plain chocolate
8 oz (225 g) butter
2 level tablespoons golden syrup
8 oz (225 g) digestive biscuits, crushed
2 oz (50 g) raisins
4 oz (110 g) toasted flaked almonds

Line two 7 inch (18 cm) baking tins with clingfilm or grease a loose-bottomed tin, because otherwise the biscuits might stick.

Break the chocolate up into very small pieces – preferably in a food processor. Place the butter, syrup and chopped chocolate in a heavy-bottomed pan over a low heat. Once melted, take the pan off the heat and allow the mixture to cool. Add the biscuit crumbs, nuts and raisins. Place the mixture into your tin and smooth the top with a palette knife. Leave until cold, then cut into twelve slices per tin.

CORNFLAKE/RICICLE SPECIALS

These will keep fresh for several days in an airtight tin.

Makes 24

Oven Temperature: 200°F, 100°C, Gas Mark $\frac{1}{4}$

4 oz (110 g) cornflakes or Ricicles
12 oz (350 g) plain chocolate
2 oz (50 g) butter or margarine

Spread the cornflakes over a shallow baking tray and put in the bottom of the oven for 10 minutes. Remove from the oven and leave until cool, then crumble them up until fairly small. They should be very crisp. Melt the chocolate and butter over a gentle heat (do not add water as this will make the cornflakes go soggy). Stir in the cornflakes and shape the mixture into small conical heaps on a greased baking tray, then leave to set.

FABULOUS FLAPJACKS

These will freeze or you can make them several days in advance and keep in an airtight tin.

Makes 12 large or 24 small

Oven Temperature: 300°F, 150°C, Gas Mark 2

8 oz (225 g) butter
5 oz (150 g) caster sugar
2 tablespoons golden syrup
10 oz (300 g) porridge oats
2 oz (50 g) raisins

Melt the butter over a low heat with the sugar and the golden syrup. Stir in the porridge oats and add the raisins. Mix well. Pour into a greased Swiss roll tin, approximately 11 × 7 inches (28 × 18 cm), and cook in the centre of the oven for 30–35 minutes until golden brown. Remove from the oven and mark into fingers. Leave to cool in the tin.

PEANUT COOKIES

Makes 36

Oven Temperature: 350°F, 180°C, Gas Mark 4

2 oz (50 g) softened butter or margarine
4 oz (110 g) brown sugar
3 tablespoons crunchy peanut butter
1 tablespoon golden syrup
1 egg
6 oz (175 g) self-raising flour

Cream the butter and sugar. Add the peanut butter and syrup and mix well. Stir in the egg, and then gradually add the flour. Take small nut-sized pieces of the dough, lightly roll in a little extra flour, then flatten them gently on a greased baking tray. Cook for 10–15 minutes – don't let them get too brown. The uncooked dough freezes very well – just wrap in clingfilm.

CHOCOLATE PRALINE CAKE

Makes 32 fingers

1 tablespoon caster sugar
4 oz (110 g) margarine
2 oz (50 g) cocoa
1 tablespoon golden syrup
8 oz (225 g) digestive biscuits, crushed
2 oz (50 g) sultanas or raisins
2 oz (50 g) walnuts, chopped
4 oz (110 g) plain chocolate
a knob of butter

Cream the sugar and the margarine together. Melt the cocoa and golden syrup together in a saucepan and add to the margarine. Stir the biscuit crumbs, sultanas and walnuts into the mixture and press down into a greased 8 inch (20 cm) square tin. Melt the chocolate with a knob of butter, and pour over the top. Leave until cold, then cut into slices.

MATCH CAKE

If you are having a match party which is also a birthday party why not round off the tea with a match cake? You will need two 8 inch (20 cm) square cakes, placed together on a board to form an oblong 16 × 8 inches (40 × 20 cm). Make the following cake recipe up twice. To ice the cake you can either use green butter icing, or apricot glaze and green glacé icing. You will also need a small quantity of white glacé icing to mark out the pitch.

Oven Temperature: 350°F, 180°C, Gas Mark 4

6 oz (175 g) soft butter or margarine
6 oz (175 g) caster sugar
a pinch of salt
grated rind and juice of $\frac{1}{2}$ orange
3 large eggs
6 oz (175 g) self-raising flour, sieved
1 tablespoon milk or water, if necessary

Grease the tin, and line the base with greased greaseproof paper, silicon paper or butter papers cut to fit.

It is very important to have your fat and eggs at room temperature and to warm your mixing bowl. Cream the fat, sugar and salt together until the ingredients are thoroughly combined and the mixture is like whipped cream. Add 1 teaspoon of the grated rind and the orange juice. Beat the eggs in a separate bowl and add them to the creamed mixture, a little at a time, beating well after each addition until the mixture returns to its fluffy state. Sift the flour into the bowl from a height, thereby allowing the flour to take in air. Carefully fold in the flour with a metal spoon. Add the milk or water if the mixture does not fall easily from the spoon. Turn the mixture into the prepared tin and bake for 45 minutes. To test if the cake is cooked, press it and if it springs back into

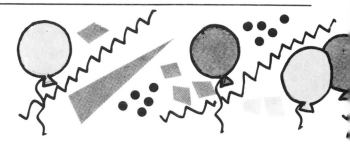

shape it is ready.

Take out of the oven, and after a minute run a palette knife along the edge of the container and turn the cake on to a wire tray. Peel off the greaseproof paper and allow to cool. See below for icings and assembly instructions.

Butter Icing

8 oz (225 g) butter, at room temperature
2 tablespoons liquid (orange juice from the other $\frac{1}{2}$ orange)
a few drops green food colouring
$1\frac{1}{4}$ lb (600 g) icing sugar, sieved

Cream the butter with a tablespoon of the liquid and the food colouring, and gradually beat in the icing sugar, and more liquid if required. Beat the mixture until the consistency is smooth and creamy.

Glacé Icing

1 lb (450 g) icing sugar, sieved
4–6 tablespoons hot water
1 tablespoon orange juice
a few drops green food colouring

Gradually mix the sieved icing sugar with the hot water, beating well until a smooth coating consistency is achieved. Add the hot water very cautiously as it is easy to make the icing too runny. When ready to use it should still seem a little stiff – this is the correct consistency. Reserve 2 tablespoons of the white glacé icing. Add the orange juice and green food colouring to the remainder.

Apricot Glaze

6 tablespoons apricot jam, sieved
2 tablespoons lemon juice

If you are using glacé icing you will need to cover the cake with a layer of apricot glaze first, to prevent the crumbs getting into the icing. Heat the jam with the lemon juice, and push through a plastic sieve into a basin with a wooden spoon. Use this mixture while still warm, but not too hot.

Match Cake Assembly

Drinking straws or construct-a-straws, cut into
* correct lengths, sellotaped together, or bent*
* into shape (for the goalposts or whatever)*
tiny plastic ball
a few players (from your local baker or use
* Subbuteo or similar, if you have them)*
candles and holders

Place the cakes on the board. Coat the sides and top of the cakes either with the green butter icing or with the apricot glaze followed by the glacé icing, and smooth with a palette knife. When the cake covering has set, pipe white lines using a fine nozzle in the appropriate positions for a simple football pitch, and stick your straws in as goal posts. Place your players on the cake and your candles around the edge of it.

This football pitch could, of course, be adapted to make a cricket, rugby or rounders pitch or a tennis court.

ICED CUP CAKES

Makes 24
Oven Temperature: 350°F, 180°C, Gas Mark 4

8 oz (225 g) butter or soft margarine
8 oz (225 g) caster sugar
4 eggs
8 oz (225 g) self-raising flour
24 paper cake cases

Icing

8 oz (225 g) icing sugar
3 or 4 tablespoons boiling water
decorations (Smarties, hundreds and
* thousands, etc)*

Beat the butter and sugar together until pale and smooth. Whisk the eggs in a separate bowl and add to the mixture a little at a time, beating all the time. Sieve the flour into the bowl and fold in. Fill the paper cases about two-thirds full, and cook for about 15 minutes, until they are well risen and golden brown.

When the cakes are quite cold, make up the icing – it should be quite stiff – and spoon it over the cakes. Smooth with a palette knife. Add the decorations, or pipe guests' names on in a contrasting colour.

Lunch and Activity Party Food

HOME-MADE BEEFBURGERS

Oven Temperature: 450°F, 230°C, Gas Mark 8

2 lb (900 g) lean beef mince
1 large onion, very finely chopped
1 tablespoon tomato sauce
1 tablespoon sweet pickle
1 heaped teaspoon tomato purée
1 teaspoon dried mixed herbs or some mixed
  herb purée
salt and freshly ground pepper

Place all the ingredients in a food processor for a couple of seconds or combine thoroughly. Form the mixture into eight thick burgers. Heat the frying pan and cook over a brisk heat turning once, or place in a hot oven and cook for 15 minutes. Serve with oven chips and peas, or in a soft roll.

PIGS IN A BLANKET

2 lb (900 g) big pork sausages
6 oz (175 g) Cheddar cheese
streaky bacon rashers

Grill the sausages for 15 minutes, then make a lengthways cut down each one and put a suitably sized slice of cheese into the cut. Grill the bacon rashers lightly (removing the rind if necessary). Wrap round the sausages and keep in place with cocktail sticks. Put under a hot grill for 5 minutes, until the bacon is crispy and the cheese has melted.

You can prepare these in advance, except for the final grilling, and leave them in the fridge. When you need them, put them under the grill for 10–15 minutes, until they are piping hot. They are also very good served cold, for a picnic or outdoor lunch.

DEVILLED CHICKEN DRUMSTICKS

A spicy recipe that older children will love.

Oven Temperature: 400°F, 200°C, Gas Mark 6

8 chicken drumsticks
$\frac{1}{4}$ pint (150 ml) vegetable oil
1 level teaspoon curry powder
1 level teaspoon paprika
$\frac{1}{2}$ level teaspoon allspice
$\frac{1}{2}$ level teaspoon ground ginger

Make a couple of shallow cuts in the flesh of each drumstick, then mix the oil and the spices. Pour the marinade over the chicken and leave for several hours, turning occasionally. Put the drumsticks in a roasting tin with the rest of the marinade and cook for 45 minutes, turning occasionally. Serve hot or cold. If you are taking them on a picnic, make sure they are completely cold before you pack them.

BACON JACKET POTATOES

Oven Temperature: 350°F, 180°C, Gas Mark 4

8 large potatoes
3 oz (75 g) butter
5 tablespoons milk
8 rashers streaky bacon
salt and freshly ground black pepper
3 oz (75 g) Cheddar cheese, grated

Clean the potatoes and bake for 1½–2 hours. Cut them in half lengthways and scoop out the middle. Mash well with the butter and milk. Grill the bacon (removing the rind if necessary) and chop it up. Add to the mashed potatoes with a little seasoning. Spoon back into the potato shells, sprinkle with grated cheese and grill until the cheese is golden and bubbly.

You can prepare these in advance except for the final grilling. When ready, give them a good 20 minutes under the grill, or 30 minutes in the oven.

LEMON PUDDING

6 oz (175 g) granulated sugar
2 heaped tablespoons plain flour
4 oz (110 g) butter
3 eggs, separated
rind and juice of 1½ large lemons
12¼ fl oz (350 ml) milk

Combine the sugar, flour, butter and egg yolks in a basin, and beat until well blended. Beat in the grated lemon rind and juice, then beat in the milk, a little at a time. Whip the egg whites until they are stiff and fold them into the mixture. Pour into an ovenproof dish, put the dish into a baking tin of hot water and cook for 30 minutes. The top should be well risen and golden, while the bottom is still runny.

CHOCOLATE MALLOWS

4 oz (110 g) plain chocolate
2 eggs, separated
1 oz (25 g) butter
20 marshmallows
1 tablespoon hot water

Melt the chocolate in a basin over hot water. Add the egg yolks, butter and marshmallows and continue to cook, stirring all the time until the mixture is smooth, then add the hot water and remove from the heat. Whisk the egg whites until they are stiff and fold into the mixture. Spoon into a serving bowl and decorate with whipped cream when it is set.

PLUM AND APPLE CRUMBLE

Oven Temperature: 350°F, 180°C, Gas Mark 4

1 lb (450 g) apples
1 lb (450 g) plums or 14 oz (400 g) can plums
sugar to taste
3 oz (75 g) butter
6 oz (175 g) flour
3 oz (75 g) demerara sugar
1 oz (25 g) walnuts or hazelnuts, chopped
* (optional)*

Peel, core and slice the apples; halve the fresh plums and take out the stones. Simmer the fruit gently in a saucepan with the sugar and a very little water until they are soft. (If you are using tinned plums, you don't need to cook them first. Simply add them to the apples [once stewed].) Make the topping by rubbing the butter into the flour until the mixture resembles fine breadcrumbs. Add the sugar and the nuts. Spread the crumble over the fruit in a baking dish and cook for 20–30 minutes. Serve hot with vanilla ice cream.

Family Party Food

STARTERS

Remember, all these recipes are for fourteen people.

Instead of actually making a course where you all need to sit down, why not simply serve 'bits' with your pre-lunch or supper drinks? The children will love helping to hand these round, so you can leave them in charge!

MINI SAUSAGE ROLLS

Makes 30

Make these the day before the party, but do heat them up for serving.

Oven Temperature: 350°F, 180°C, Gas Mark 4

3 oz (75 g) butter (but do not cut it off the block)
4½ oz (125 g) self-raising flour
1½ dessertspoons water
or
12 oz (350 g) packet JusRol flaky pastry
6 oz (175 g) sausagemeat
a little milk

Use a block of very cold butter: better still, put it in the freezer for 2 hours. Unwrap one end of the block and mark off a 3 oz (75 g) section. Sift a little flour into a bowl and grate the butter coarsely on top of the flour. Add more flour and then butter, and continue until both are used up. Mix together very gently with a metal spoon until the mixture resembles fine breadcrumbs, then add water to mix. The finished mixture should feel light and require no kneading.

Roll out into a rectangle on a floured board, again very gently, and cut into two strips lengthways. Divide the sausagemeat into two halves, and roll with your hands into two sausages, the same length as the pastry. Brush the long edge of the pastry with milk, and lay the sausagemeat down the length of the pastry and bring up the edges to the centre to cover the sausagemeat. Press the edges firmly together, making an indented edge with your fingertips, and brush the pastry with milk. Place on a greased baking tray, cut into rolls 1 inch (2.5 cm) long, and cook for 15 minutes.

Reduce the oven temperature to 350°F, 180°C, Gas Mark 4, and cook for a further 10 minutes, but do not let them get too brown. They should rise well and be deep gold to light brown in colour.

DIPS AND BITS

Dips (see page 77).

Grapes stuffed with cream cheese: use white or black grapes (see page 95).

Celery stuffed with cream cheese (see page 95).

Radishes with cream cheese:
Choose large radishes and halve them horizontally. Cut off the tops and bottoms to allow them to stand firmly on a plate. Pipe a rosette of seasoned cream cheese on each half. For a Valentine Party, use a heart-shaped aspic cutter to cut tiny radish skin hearts and place one on each rosette.

CHEESE STRAWS

You can make these in the traditional cheese-straw shape or use cutters in the shape of animals, ducks, hearts, stars, etc., to make them look more interesting. Make them up to a week in advance, but store in an airtight tin and reheat if necessary to crisp them.

Makes 64
Oven Temperature: 350°F, 180°C, Gas Mark 4

4 oz (110 g) plain flour
1 teaspoon salt
2 oz (50 g) butter
2 oz (50 g) Cheddar cheese, grated
1 egg yolk
1 tablespoon cold water

Sift the flour and salt together and rub in the butter to give a texture like fine breadcrumbs. Stir in the cheese and egg yolk, and add enough cold water to give a stiff dough, but be careful not to add too much. Roll the pastry thinly and if you are making straws trim to 8 inch (20 cm) squares. Put on a greased baking tray and cut into straws, 2 inch (5 cm) long and ½ inch (1 cm) wide, separating them gently with the knife. If you are using cutters, cut out shapes before putting them on the tray. Bake in the centre of the oven for 10–15 minutes, until golden.

POPCORN

Children enjoy helping to make popcorn, because the results are so spectacular, and a little corn makes a great deal of popcorn.

3 oz (75 g) popping corn
2 tablespoons cooking oil
2 tablespoons sugar or 1 tablespoon salt

Heat the oil until it is lightly smoking in a large heavy-bottomed saucepan with a tightly fitting lid. Add the popcorn, one kernel deep in the bottom of the pan, and shake it well while it is cooking. Keep the lid on! When it has finished popping, put it into bowls, sprinkle with the salt or sugar, and leave to cool slightly before handing it round.

MAIN COURSES

MEAT FONDUE

Allow ½ lb (225 g) of meat per adult in total, and as far as the children are concerned, don't forget that a fourteen-year-old chap will eat as much as a father, if not more! So gauge the amount of meat you allow for the children according to their ages.

Have a selection of diced meats – chicken breast, sausages, steak, the best you can afford. Remember that although you are not actually cooking the meat, it does take a long time to dice. Make sure you have a good sharp knife. Try to avoid having frozen meat as it will spit more in the fondue because of the higher water content.

Chicken, sausage and pork should be cooked longer than the steak, and beware of spitting sausages too!

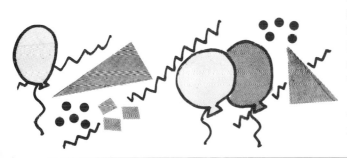

FONDUE SAUCES

Do not make enormous quantities of each sauce, say $\frac{1}{2}$ pint (275 ml) of each. Have these on the serving table, and everyone can put a selection on their plates which will avoid stretching over and accidents happening.

Curry:
Mix mayonnaise with a little curry powder or curry paste to taste. Add a little lemon juice if you wish.

Tomato:
Mix mayonnaise with a tablespoon of tomato purée.

Mayonnaise:
With chopped chives, chopped parsley, lemon juice and whipped cream. Whip the cream. Add to the mayonnaise with the other ingredients and mix well.

Salad Cream:
Just plain for the children's sake – amazingly, some love it with anything and everything.

Barbecue Sauce:
See page 69.

Horseradish Sauce:
Don't try to make your own, buy a bottle and, if it is very hot, add some double cream.

Allow one fondue set per six people maximum. Your friends will not mind bringing theirs with them. Heat the containers of oil on the hob in the kitchen first, but be very careful of bringing them through to your dining area, and don't have children running around. Put them in the centre of the table out of harm's way – do remember to get enough fuel for the fondue before the party. Keep an eye on the sets used by the children to make sure they are not overheating. Test to make sure that the oil is hot enough by putting some diced bread in it. If it cooks fast and furiously you will know the temperature is correct. Serve some diced white bread together with some sliced mushrooms (allow one per person) for the children to pop in with their meat, as it will be delicious fried (French bread does not fry as well as ordinary bread).

No-one should try to eat from their cooking fork – do remind the children – as it would burn them.

COLD CHICKEN CONCOCTION
(with selection of cold meats)

3 × 3$\frac{1}{2}$ lb (1.5 kg) chickens, cooked

Sauce
$\frac{1}{2}$ pint (275 ml) mayonnaise
$\frac{3}{4}$ pint (425 ml) cream
$\frac{1}{4}$ pint (150 ml) yoghurt
2 tablespoons curry paste
1 tablespoon apricot jam, sieved
1–1$\frac{1}{2}$ tablespoons coconut cream
3–4 fresh peaches or nectarines
juice of 1 lemon
chopped parsley

Cook your chickens (we recommend simmering with onion, carrot, bay leaf, 6 peppercorns and water and/or wine for 1$\frac{1}{2}$ hours), then allow to cool in the liquid. Drain and strip off all the flesh (freeze the stock for use in a soup later). Keep some of the flesh separate, wrap in clingfilm and refrigerate (in case any children do not like curry sauce). For the sauce, mix the mayonnaise, cream, yoghurt, curry paste, apricot jam and coconut cream in the blender. Add the chicken and refrigerate.

Take the mixture out of the fridge an hour before serving to allow the flavour to develop.

Slice peeled peaches or nectarines and sprinkle and mix with lemon juice. Fold into the chicken and sprinkle with the chopped parsley.

BEEF CASSEROLE

Oven Temperature: 325°F, 160°C, Gas Mark 3

5 lb (2.25 kg) chuck steak, diced
4 tablespoons cooking oil
3 onions, diced
6 slices bacon, chopped
6 slices carrot
2 sticks celery, sliced
4 oz (110 g) mushrooms, sliced
5 heaped tablespoons flour
2½ pints (1.5 litres) good jellied stock (if possible, otherwise use stock cubes)
wine (optional, and cut down the stock if you do use wine)
oregano or mixed herbs to taste
salt and freshly ground pepper

Cut your meat into bite-sized cubes and fry fast in the oil in a flameproof casserole. Remove the meat when browned all over and fry onions over a gentler heat. When the onion is transparent, add the bacon and fry for a few minutes, then add all the other vegetables. Once these are softened check and see if you need a little more oil, and then sprinkle on the flour. Cook for a few minutes and gradually add the stock and/or wine, herbs and seasoning. Put the meat back into the casserole, and bring to the boil slowly. Taste the sauce and adjust the seasoning, and put in the oven for 2–2½ hours until the meat is tender. You may need to use two casserole dishes, as this recipe is for a large quantity.

SALAD

SALAD FOR 14

Try honey instead of sugar in your dressing – it's delicious and practically drunk separately by the children in our family.

2 large lettuces, or 2 different sorts of lettuce (1 round and 1 Chinese leaf, etc.)
3 large oranges, sliced
3 kiwi fruit, sliced
1 cucumber, sliced
1 bunch or packet watercress
1 green and 1 red pepper, sliced
1 head celery, chopped
chopped parsley
½ pint (275 ml) salad dressing

If you have a large bowl which will be suitable for salad, the easiest way to make sure that everybody gets a bit of everything is to make layers of the salad: start off with a bed of lettuce and cover it with one of the sliced oranges, one of the kiwi fruit, a few slices of cucumber and some of the watercress, peppers and chopped celery. Sprinkle on some parsley, then follow with the same layers again, so that in the end you will have about three layers altogether. Do not toss the salad in case some of the younger children would prefer not to have a dressing. Serve that separately, in a jug.

Drinks

Here we give drink recipes for every kind of party, from sophisticated sounding 'cocktails' for teenage discos and suppers, to sparkling thirst-quenchers for younger age groups and satisfying milk shakes for smaller parties.

The first big question with older children is the problem of alcohol. It is important to discuss this openly with your own children when you are planning the party. Remember that when you were young you wanted to experiment, and your children will too. But they must realise that as a parent you will have to keep a very close watch on what everyone is drinking. During the party you will be responsible not only for your own children but for all their guests as well. You must insist that people do not bring drink in with them, so don't be afraid to take it away if you see any evidence of extra alcohol. You can agree with your older children to serve a limited amount of alcohol at the party in exchange for nobody bringing their own. Then you can quietly reduce or cut out the alcohol after everyone has had their first glass.

By this stage children love to feel sophisticated so it is very important to give the drinks exciting and grown-up names, even if the content is totally innocuous. Dress up the concoctions with sliced fruit, ice and colouring, and the glasses (for a small party) with frosting, cocktail umbrellas or other decorations (see page 20).

The suggested recipes are all subject to your own taste, so mix and adjust them to suit yourself and your children. Always have a trial tasting well before the party. Perhaps the children could organise this, but be prepared for a messy kitchen.

With regard to quantities you will find that a 1 litre bottle will be sufficient for nine wine glasses. A bottle of wine (75 cl) will give seven wine glasses. Adapt these recipes to fit your numbers, but remember that children drink a lot at parties, particularly when being very active.

HARVEST PUNCH

A good 'cup' for larger parties.

1 carton apple juice
½ × 2½ pint (1.5 litre) bottle cider
2 × 2½ pint (1.5 litre) bottles lemonade
sliced fruit
mint, if available

Mix all the liquid ingredients together, then add the chopped fruit and mint. Add ice direct to glasses. When refilling, use either less cider, or if preferred no more cider, but increase the proportion of apple juice. For a non-alcoholic cup omit the cider altogether and increase the apple juice (see page 17).

BUCKS FIZZLE

1 carton fresh orange juice
1 × 2½ pint (1.5 litre) bottle lemonade
slices of orange

Mix the ingredients together, and serve immediately.

BUCKS FIZZ

2 cartons fresh orange juice
1 bottle sparkling white wine
1 bottle sparkling non-alcoholic wine or grape
 juice
slices of orange

Chill all the ingredients very thoroughly. Mix together and serve at once. When refilling, increase quantity of non-alcoholic wine, or see above for non-alcoholic recipe.

CHAMPAGNE COCKTAIL

1 bottle sparkling wine
1 bottle sparkling non alcoholic wine or grape
 juice
sugar lumps
brandy essence

Chill the wine very thoroughly. Put a sugar lump in each glass and one or two drops of brandy essence. Either mix the non-alcoholic and alcoholic wines together to serve if you wish your guests only to have half a glass of wine, or fill each glass with the sparkling wine then refill with non-alcoholic.

KIR

(for pink parties)

1 bottle dry white wine
1 bottle non-alcoholic wine or grape juice
Ribena

Chill the wine thoroughly. Pour a little Ribena into the bottom of each glass and fill up as above, either with a mixture of the non-alcoholic and alcoholic wines, or start with the wine and refill with the non-alcoholic wine. Serve at once.

ROYAL KIR

(for pink parties)

1 bottle sparkling white wine or grape juice
1 bottle non-alcoholic white wine
strawberry syrup as used in milk shakes

Chill the wine thoroughly. Put a little strawberry syrup in the bottom of each glass and fill up as above.

PINK POTION

(for pink parties)

1 × 3½ pint (2 litre) bottle of lemonade
strawberry syrup or cochineal food colouring

Chill the lemonade thoroughly. Pour a little strawberry syrup or food colouring in each glass and fill up with lemonade. Serve at once.

GREEN GIGGLES

(for green parties)

1 × 3½ pint (2 litre) bottle of lemonade
green food colouring

Chill lemonade thoroughly. Pour a couple of drops of food colouring in each glass and fill up with lemonade. Serve on a tray immediately, or pour quite a few drops of green food colouring into a jug and fill up with lemonade. Watch out for green mouths! Serve at once.

LIME COCKTAIL

(for green parties)

1 × 3½ pint (2 litre) bottle of lemonade
lime concentrate

Chill lemonade thoroughly. Pour some
concentrate in the glasses and fill with
lemonade, or make up a jug. Serve at once.

GREEN LIGHT GO-GO

(for green parties)

1 bottle sparkling white wine
1 bottle non-alcoholic white wine or grape juice
green food colouring

Chill the wine thoroughly. Put a couple of drops
of food colouring in each glass and fill up with
white wine and refill with the non-alcoholic
wine, or just half a glass of wine and half of
grape juice. Serve at once.

TROPICAL PUNCH

1 carton tropical fruit juice
1 bottle sparkling wine
1 bottle sparkling non-alcoholic wine or grape
  juice
slices of kiwi fruit, mango or other tropical fruit

Chill all ingredients and mix together. Serve at
once.

TROPICAL TREAT

1 carton tropical fruit juice
1 bottle Perrier
slices of fruit as above

Chill all the ingredients and mix together. Serve
at once.

SANGRIA

1 bottle dry white or medium dry wine, or 1
  box of grape juice
1 bottle Perrier
sliced fruit

Chill all ingredients and mix together. Serve at
once.

RED SANGRIA

6 lemons
2 oz (50 g) sugar
1 bottle red wine
1 × 3½ pint (2 litre) bottle lemonade

Slice the lemons and put in a bowl with the
sugar. Leave for 24 hours then squeeze and
strain. Mix the wine and lemonade and add the
strained lemon juice.

SPRITZER

1 bottle dry or medium dry white wine
soda water

Chill the ingredients and mix together. (Put in
more soda than wine for younger children.)
Serve immediately.

PIMMS

Pimms
lemonade
sliced fruit
mint

We have not specified quantities for this recipe
as it depends on the age of your guests. Serve
this with a drop of Pimms to the younger and
a stronger mix, if you want, for the older
children, and weaken as necessary for refills.

MULLED MYSTERY

8 fl oz (225 ml) Ribena
3½ pints (2 litres) orange juice
3 oranges, each stuck with 6 cloves
1 teaspoon ground cinnamon
red wine (optional)

Place all the ingredients in a heavy-based saucepan and allow to simmer gently for 30 minutes. It does *not* taste of pure Ribena! Serve hot after a cold outing, like a fireworks party. Have prepared beforehand and heat up when you get in.

WINE CUP

This wine cup is alcoholic. It is included in case you need a drink for much older teenagers. As the evening progresses increase the lemonade in the mix.

1 × 2½ pint (1.5 litre) bottle lemonade
1 × 2½ pint (1.5 litre) bottle cider
1 bottle white wine
a scant pint (500 ml) grape juice
⅛ bottle orange Curaçao

Mix all the ingredients together.

HOME-MADE LEMONADE

4 lemons
4 tablespoons sugar
3 pints (1.7 litres) boiling water
10 ice cubes

Cut the lemons into quarters. Put them with the sugar into a heat-resistant jug. Pour on the boiling water and leave to stand for thirty minutes. Strain, cool, add the ice cubes and serve.

HOME-MADE ORANGEADE

Follow the recipe for lemonade as above. When it is cool, squeeze the juice of 4 oranges into the lemonade, add the ice cubes and serve.

SPARKLING APPLE PUNCH

2 red-skinned eating apples
juice of 1 lemon
2 large oranges
1 large bottle concentrated apple juice
2 pints (1.1 litre) soda or tonic water
2 pints (1.1 litre) dry ginger ale

Wash and dry the apples, then quarter, core and slice them. Pour lemon juice over them to stop them going brown. Slice the oranges into small pieces, discarding the pips. Place the apple juice and prepared fruits into a large bowl. Cover and chill for about 2 hours. Chill the soda or tonic water and ginger ale. Just before serving measure out soda or tonic water and ginger ale and combine with the apple juice. Ladle into glasses for serving.

SPARKLING FRUIT BOWL PUNCH

2 red-skinned eating apples
lemon juice
2 large oranges
½ lb (225 g) grapes
fresh strawberries or raspberries, if in season
2 pints (1.1 litre) soda water
2 pints (1.1 litre) ginger ale
1 large cup concentrated fruit syrup (as used in milk shakes)

Follow the recipe as above.

HOME-MADE BLENDER LEMONADE

4 thin-skinned lemons
4 tablespoons sugar
10 ice cubes
3 pints (1.7 litres) cold water

Cut the lemons into quarters. Put all the ingredients, reserving 2 pints (1.1 litre) of water and 5 ice cubes, into the blender and blend for 10 seconds. Strain, add remaining water and ice cubes and serve.

FIZZY APPLE PUNCH

½ pint (300 ml) concentrated apple juice
2 pints (1.1 litre) soda water
2 pints (1.1 litre) ginger ale
2 eating apples (red if possible)

Chill all the ingredients (except the apples) for 2 hours. Quarter and core the apples, but do not peel them, and cut the quarters into small chunks. Put into a large jug. Pour over the other ingredients and serve.

FIZZY APRICOT PUNCH

2 lemons
1 × 10 oz (275 g) can apricots (stoned)
3 pints (1.7 litres) fizzy lemonade

Chill all the ingredients for at least 2 hours. Cut the lemons into quarters, and put into a blender with the apricots. Blend for 20 seconds. Strain into a serving jug, and mix well with ½ pint (300 ml) lemonade. Add the rest of the lemonade, and serve.

FIZZY ORANGE PUNCH

1 pint (570 ml) orange juice
2 pints (1.1 litre) tonic water
10 ice cubes
a few orange slices

Chill the ingredients in the fridge for at least 2 hours. Pour the orange juice into a jug. Mix well with ½ pint (300 ml) of the tonic water. Add the rest of the tonic water, the ice cubes, the slices of orange, and serve.

COLA SURPRISE

3 pints (1.7 litres) Coca-Cola or Pepsi-Cola
small carton of ice cream

Spoon or scoop the ice cream into each serving glass. Pour the Cola over and serve.

PINEAPPLE DREAM

1 × 10 oz (275 g) can pineapple chunks
2 pints (1.1 litre) cold milk
vanilla ice cream

Put the pineapple, its juice and 1 pint (570 ml) milk into the liquidizer, and blend for 20 seconds. Add remaining milk. Pour into serving glasses and top with a scoopful of vanilla ice cream. Serve with straws.

BANANA WHIZ

2 bananas
1 egg
2 pints (1.1 litre) cold milk
1 tablespoon sugar
chocolate vermicelli

Peel the bananas, chop, and put in the blender. Break the egg into the blender and add the other ingredients, reserving 1 pint (570 ml) of milk. Blend for 20 seconds until foaming. Add the remaining milk. Pour into tall glasses and serve with straws. Just before serving sprinkle with vermicelli.

CHOCOLATE BANANA SHAKE

2 bananas
2 pints (1.1 litre) cold milk
2 heaped tablespoons drinking chocolate or 1
  tablespoon each cocoa and sugar

Peel the bananas, chop, and put into the blender. Add the other ingredients, reserving 1 pint (570 ml) of milk, and blend for 20 seconds until foamy. Add remaining milk. Pour into tall glasses and serve with straws.

BLACKCURRANT DELIGHT

5 tablespoons Ribena
2 pints (1.1 litre) cold milk
vanilla ice cream
hundreds and thousands

Mix the Ribena and milk together. Pour into tall glasses. Top with a scoop of vanilla ice cream and just before serving sprinkle with hundreds and thousands. Serve with straws.

PEPPERMINT DELIGHT

a few drops peppermint essence
a few drops green colouring
1 tablespoon sugar
2 pints (1.1 litre) cold milk
soft ice cream

Add the peppermint essence, green colouring and sugar to the cold milk, and stir well. Pour into tall glasses and top with a scoop of ice cream.

APRICOT DELIGHT

1 × 10 oz (275 g) can apricots (stoned)
1 tablespoon sugar
2 pints (1.1 litre) milk
6 ice cubes

Put all the ingredients into a blender, reserving 1 pint (570 ml) milk, and blend for 20 seconds. Add remaining milk. Pour into tall glasses and serve with straws.

RASPBERRY SODA

8 oz (225 g) fresh or frozen raspberries
2 pints (1.1 litre) milk
1 small bottle tonic water
1 small block of Raspberry Ripple ice cream

Partially defrost the frozen raspberries. Put the raspberries and 1 pint (570 ml) milk into a blender and blend for 20 seconds. Strain. Add remaining milk and tonic water. Pour into serving glasses. Top with a scoop of ice cream.

Home-Made Sweets for Presents

Sweets are really quite easy to make and are popular presents. Wrap four or five sweets together in a 6 inch (15 cm) square of clingfilm or cellophane and tie with freezer ties and colourful narrow ribbons. Remember that you could also use these to serve with coffee after a party for older children: put the green peppermint creams on the table following the green party; serve dark chocolate truffles following the black and white party; and pink coconut ice for pink parties . . .

FUDGE

1 lb (450 g) sugar
5 oz (150 g) butter
¼ pint (150 ml) milk

Grease a tin about 8 inches (20 cm) square. Put all the ingredients into a saucepan over a gentle heat and stir until the sugar is dissolved. Bring to the boil, stirring all the time, and boil until a small spoonful of the mixture dropped into a cup of cold water forms a ball. Take off the heat and beat for a couple of moments until the mixture has cooled slightly. Pour into the tin and cut into squares when cold.

CHOCOLATE FUDGE

Make as above, adding 2 tablespoons cocoa, and make sure the cocoa is completely dissolved before the mixture comes to the boil.

VERY EASY CHOCOLATE FUDGE

A very quick and easy recipe. It doesn't need cooking, so children can make it themselves, but it tastes just like the real thing.

10 oz (275 g) icing sugar
3 oz (75 g) cream cheese
3 oz (75 g) plain chocolate, broken up
3 level tablespoons cocoa
2 oz (50 g) raisins or chopped walnuts
  (optional)

Sieve the icing sugar and mix well with the cream cheese. Melt the chocolate with the cocoa in a basin over hot water. Mix into the cheese and add the raisins or nuts. Line a 7 inch (18 cm) square tin and spread the fudge, smoothing it with a palette knife dipped into boiling water. Put it in the fridge and cut it into squares when it is set. The fudge will keep for at least a month if you store it in the fridge.

TOFFEE APPLES

6–8 unblemished eating apples
1 lb (450 g) demerara sugar
2 oz (50 g) butter
¼ pint (150 ml) water
2 tablespoons golden syrup
1 wooden stick per apple (or lolly stick)

First of all prepare your apples; wipe them clean, dry them and insert the sticks. In a large heavy-bottomed pan melt the remaining ingredients over a gentle heat (do not stir too much as this may cause the toffee to crystallise). When the sugar has dissolved, boil rapidly for about 5 minutes. If you have a sugar thermometer, boil until the temperature is 290°F (143°C), otherwise test the toffee by popping a little into cold water – it should set quite hard. Remove the pan from the heat. Tipping it slightly, dip in your apples and coat each one completely. Stand the apples either on a buttered tray or on wax paper. When quite cold, wrap each one in a piece of cellophane, clingfilm or waxed paper, and fasten with ribbon or freezer twists ties. You can prepare these toffee apples a couple of days before the party but keep them somewhere dry.

PEANUT AND CHOCOLATE BALLS

3½ oz (100 g) plain chocolate, broken up
1 oz (25 g) butter
2 oz (50 g) peanuts
1 teaspoon vanilla essence

Put the chocolate in a bowl and stand over heated hot water. Add the butter and leave until both are melted. Chop the peanuts coarsely and add to the chocolate with the vanilla essence. Form into balls, and leave to firm before wrapping.

COCONUT ICE

1 lb (450 g) sugar
¼ pint (150 ml) milk
5 oz (150 g) desiccated coconut
pink food colouring

Grease a tin, 8 inches (20 cm) square. Put the sugar and milk into a saucepan and heat gently until the sugar has dissolved. Bring to the boil, stirring continuously, and cook until a spoonful dropped into cold water forms a soft ball. Remove from the heat and stir in the coconut. Pour half the mixture into the tin, add pink colouring to the remaining half, and then pour over the first portion. Divide into 1 inch (2.5 cm) squares, while the coconut ice is cooling. Don't take out of the tin until completely cold.

PEPPERMINT CREAMS

If you like leave half the mixture plain and make a mixture of green and white peppermint creams, or pink and white if you use pink food colouring.

10 oz (275 g) icing sugar, sieved
1 egg white, stiffly beaten
a few drops of peppermint essence
green or pink food colouring

Add the sieved icing sugar to the whisked egg white, and mix with a wooden spoon (if not stiff enough add a little extra icing sugar). Stir in the peppermint essence and green food colouring. Roll out peppermint mixture on to a board sprinkled with icing sugar and cut out shapes (diamonds, stars, etc) with a knife, the smallest size pastry cutter, or a suitably sized lid. Leave the peppermints in a cool place until they are set hard (this may take several hours).

ROSIE'S CHOCOLATE TRUFFLES

8 oz (225 g) good quality plain chocolate,
 broken up
4 oz (110 g) unsalted butter
8 oz (225 g) sieved icing sugar
4 fl oz (100 ml) double cream
4 tablespoons ground almonds
2 tablespoons brandy, rum or orange juice
Cocoa

Melt the chocolate in a double boiler. Mix in all the other ingredients, excepting the cocoa. Pour into a bowl and leave to cool in the fridge. Wash your hands in very cold water, and form the mixture into balls. Put some cocoa on a plate and roll the balls in it. Leave overnight in the fridge before you wrap them, if you are giving them as presents. If serving with coffee then put into little petits-fours cases. Store them in an airtight tin in the fridge. You can make these a couple of days before you need them.

BISCUITS TO HANG ON A CHRISTMAS TREE

1 recipe Shortbread (see page 106)
star or suitable Christmas shaped cutters
$\frac{1}{4}$–$\frac{1}{2}$ inch (5–10 mm) diameter circular cutter
 (even a pencil would do)
very narrow ribbon or parcel ribbon

Roll out the shortbread mixture and cut into shapes. Before cooking, make a hole in the top of each biscuit, through which you can put the hanging ribbon. You do not want the hole to be too near an edge or the shortbread will break, and you want it centrally positioned so that the shape will hang properly and not be overweighted on one side. Decorate your shape with icing and silver balls if you wish.

General Index

Recipe Index

Picture credits
Tony Stone (opp. p. 33)
Vision International (centre spread, Anthea Sieveking left).